Contents

Introduction: The Puzzle of the Will

I bring my fourteen-year-old son to a meeting with his Spanish teacher. She seems to be an effective teacher who wants the best for my son. He has been diagnosed with ADHD, and has a C in her class. She has made some accommodations for my son's disorder in accordance with an individual plan my wife and I asked the school to make. Here is what the teacher tells me:

"Your son has a real facility with language, both in grammar and in pronunciation. He does well on tests. He would be great in Honors Spanish next year. I would hate to see him in regular Spanish, but he needs an A-minus to qualify for Honors. I know he has ADD . . . the reason he has a C is he turns in assignments late or forgets to turn them in at all. Also, his mind often seems to be elsewhere during class. He could get an A if he would try harder. He has to want it badly enough."

I wonder to myself about the teacher's appraisal. Let's consider this as a multiple-choice question:

Is the teacher correct?

A) Yes, my son could get an A if he tried harder.

B) No, my son has a disability, so he cannot get an A by trying harder. He needs more accommodations from the school.

C) There are not enough facts to make a determination.

Choosing answer A risks committing an injustice by demanding that my son perform a task that his disability prevents him from completing. Choosing answer B may undersell his ability, inhibiting him from reaching his full potential —and giving him an unrealistic picture of what will be expected of him going forward in life. The safe choice here is answer C, because it only requires looking for more facts before making a decision. But C raises a question: If we need more facts, what facts would be sufficient?

Russell Barkley, a clinical psychologist and clinical professor of psychiatry, is perhaps the foremost expert on Attention-Deficit/Hyperactivity Disorder (ADHD). He theorizes that ADHD is a problem with executive functioning in his book, *ADHD and the Nature of Self-Control,* and elsewhere. People with the disorder act impulsively, seem distracted, have trouble staying on task, forget things, and have difficulty with planning and organization. Psychologists once called it ADD, and this remains its colloquial name, which I will use on occasion throughout this book.

Barkley, or any other expert, would label the behavior the Spanish teacher describes as textbook ADHD. But it could equally be the behavior of a typical boy who doesn't care too much about getting an A in Spanish right now, or dislikes the work and lacks the will to do it. A child with ADHD might also, like a typical child, dislike a class or lack the will to work at it. It could be this, rather than the ADHD, that is decisive. So while the teacher's account seems uncharitable, it is not obviously wrong. What facts would truly settle the matter?

If we were to go along with the teacher by choosing A and the boy was successful, we would then know that trying harder was enough—and that this alone sufficed to achieve a positive outcome. But that doesn't quite satisfy. We want to know *now*, not later. It may also make us wonder if he really had ADHD in the first place. That outcome resolves the problem, but it leaves the larger puzzle intact.

Other than this happy result, I cannot think of one fact or a set of facts that would settle the matter conclusively. Beneath this question lies a serious gap in assumptions. The teacher assumes that a student with ADD could lessen some of his symptoms by an effort of will. But many advocates for people with ADD believe that because the disorder is real, it is wrong to expect a mere effort of will to result in change.

The problem is that this disorder can be real while its symptoms can, at times, respond to efforts of will. Like my son, I have ADD. While I continue to suffer from its symptoms after 47 years of living with it, I can also report that I have been able to suppress its symptoms on occasion by an effort of will. If I made fewer attempts to suppress symptoms, I would display more of them. I could conceivably make more attempts at suppression, and display fewer symptoms. So how do we know which symptoms, at which times, might yield to a properly engaged will, and which could not? Most of us believe, like the Spanish teacher, that each individual becomes who they are in part by mustering their will and channeling it in a direction of their own choosing. ADD frustrates this effort, but by how much and when? Are there moments when no willful effort could suppress symptoms? How can we separate the moments when the ADD is expressing itself through our behavior from the moments when our behavior is our own? This is the puzzle of the will.

The puzzle in my family

The problem of the will does not merely frustrate attempts to calibrate academic expectations. Those with ADD face challenges in every sphere of life. At home, when my wife and I watch our son procrastinate instead of writing a report for school, we grow frustrated. It is true that procrastination comes with ADD, but when we direct his attention to the fact that he is procrastinating, and he still refuses to start working, we incline toward viewing him as a willing procrastinator. It is hard to see him, on those occasions, as an unfortunate sufferer of a disorder that makes him procrastinate. Once we view him as a willing procrastinator, we become resentful. Why won't he do what we need him to do?

One might hope that I would understand my son, since I have ADD myself. Unfortunately, I don't even know how to appraise my own behavior. I was first diagnosed and medicated in the 1970s for what was then called "hyperactivity." One way the disorder complicates my life is in my relationship with my wife. For example, my wife and I recently had a dispute, at the end of a long day, about what we would make for dinner. We had little food in the house, and I made the observation that this was because my wife had declined to go shopping with me on the weekend. This may have been true, but casting blame interferes with problem solving. What's more, I might have done well to remember that my wife had announced the onset of PMS the day before. The combination of hunger and PMS does not dispose my wife to entertain criticism gracefully.

All this is easy to see in hindsight. Had I put just one or two of these facts together prior to speaking, and reflected upon them, I would have behaved differently. I would have kept quiet and searched for food with the earnestness of one seeking to appease a foraging bear at a picnic. But to do that, I would have needed to refrain from speaking while I considered the likely consequences of what I was about to say. But the ability to think before I act is precisely the behavior that my ADHD frustrates.

This behavior—refraining from behavior long enough to think about it—is what Russell Barkley calls "inhibiting prepotent response." A prepotent response is immediate behavior a subject is disposed or conditioned to display —in laymen's terms, a first impulse. Barkley theorizes that the entire problem of ADHD stems from difficulty at inhibiting first impulses (*ADHD and the Nature of Self-Control* 47). When we fail to inhibit our impulses, we cannot employ and develop our executive functions. Executive functions govern things like keeping track of time, staying on a task, fulfilling a behavioral goal across time, regulating emotional and motivational states, and foreseeing the consequences of certain behaviors (*ADHD and the Nature of Self-Control* 209–217). Such as, say, foreseeing what happens when you criticize your wife when she is hungry and pre-menstrual.

Like my son's Spanish teacher, though, we might be skeptical that my disorder really controlled my behavior on this occasion. Some husbands who do not suffer from ADHD also blame their wives when things go wrong. They might do this to deflect their own self-blaming tendencies, or to exercise control over their wives, or because this is a behavior their own father modeled. Colloquially, we might say these men are being jerks. This is where I face the same problem of appraisal with regard to myself as I face with my son. Maybe I was not really suffering from ADHD at that moment. Maybe I was just being a jerk.

Unlikely, Unable, or Unwilling?

This sort of conundrum is, for me, the puzzle of ADHD. It has been obscured, rather than illuminated, by tedious arguments about whether or not the disorder is "real." Nor is this a puzzle that researchers have been eager to tackle directly. Barkley, for example, in his most recent scholarly book, *Executive Functions: What They Are, How They Work, and Why They Evolved*, refers explicitly to this problem exactly once. He does so in the final chapter. To my knowledge, it is his most candid admission of the issue. His reference to it comes in the form of one sentence that notes the trouble mental health and education professionals have coping with executive function disorders like ADHD. "At the core of such problems," Barkley says, "is the vexing issue of just how one gets people to behave in ways that even they know may be good for them when they seem unlikely, unable or unwilling to perform" (200). His phrasing captures the puzzle succinctly: Are we merely *unlikely*, absolutely *unable*, or simply *unwilling* to perform? If Barkley were able to prove that people with ADHD are *unable* at all times to perform those tasks they characteristically struggle with, this would be a very different disorder, and we would regard it differently. But Barkley includes the word "unwilling" on this list. In doing so, he acknowledges the possibility that my son's Spanish teacher could be right when she thinks my son may not to *want to succeed badly enough*, or that I fear when I wonder if I am just being a jerk for criticizing my wife at inappropriate moments.

While Barkley has contributed an admirable phrase that captures the problem, he misses a key aspect of the issue. He describes the uncertainty about whether the disordered are *unlikely, unable, or unwilling* as "vexing" for mental health and education professionals. But he doesn't consider whether it might be vexing for the attention disordered themselves, or for those close to them. As someone with the disorder, I would like to assure him that I am pretty damned vexed.

Those of us living with ADD live know we are *unlikely* to perform as others do. After we act, we often feel we were *unable* to avoid displaying symptomatic behavior. When we are called to account for behavior we feel *unable* to have avoided, we feel persecuted and misunderstood. Often, though, we harbor a suspicion that we might have actually been *unwilling* to perform on a particular occasion. Perhaps we didn't want to perform, or didn't want to perform badly enough, or even held a self-deceptive belief about our own willingness to perform. When that happens, we feel guilty and ashamed. But since it may have just been our disorder after all, we also feel confused. How we feel about a particular instance of behavior depends on whether we believe our symptoms were acting up—or *we* were.

We cannot separate a symptom from a lapse of will in a definitive way. As a result, when someone else's attribution of intention conflicts with our own, we don't know whether to feel persecuted or ashamed. This is our puzzle. For those who live with the disorder every day and hope for help from mental health and education professionals, this puzzle represents an under-examined aspect of ADHD.

At root, ADHD creates a puzzle about personal responsibility. Our society believes in the principle that we should only assign moral blame to people for behavior that they control. But in the case of ADHD, we don't know how to draw a line between what particular instances of behavior *we* control and what instances *are controlled by our disorder*. This is hardly a trivial problem, because life demands the drawing of such lines every day.

1 — The Funny Problem We Get When We Call It a Disorder

When people argue about whether or not the disorder is "real," they may really be trying to get at the problem of personal responsibility. Russell Barkley thinks so, contending that society views self-control as a moral problem, and that this "helps explain why the widespread social acceptance of ADHD as a disability has been so difficult to attain" (*ADHD and the Nature of Self-Control* 319). Those who insist that ADHD is not a real disorder will always choose answer A on the multiple-choice question in my story. Denying the disorder preserves the notion of moral or personal responsibility: If ADHD isn't even a disorder, it cannot control behavior. Advocates like Barkley would incline toward answer B, because if a disorder is real, we should not blame someone for exhibiting symptoms of it. All too often, those with ADHD and their loved ones find themselves in the everlasting purgatory of answer C.

So deciding once and for all that ADHD is a "real" disorder might seem to hold the promise of resolving this puzzle for the benefit of the disordered. It cannot do so. The hope would be that proving the disorder to be real would exonerate those who suffer from it. But in daily life, the coin of this promised exoneration is not fungible. Even when most people accept the reality of our disorder—which is already the case in many parts of the United States—they still wonder if we might succeed by trying a little harder, and they still often resent us for our failings. We who suffer from the disorder have similar doubts, even though we feel sure we are different from other people. A close look at the "reality of the disorder" debate shows why it cannot help us live with this puzzle.

One way to think about what it means to have a disorder is to compare it to other disorders with less-questioned pedigrees. We might ask those who blame the attention disordered for their behavior, for example, if they would also blame epileptics for their seizures. The point of this analogy is that if both epilepsy and ADHD are real disorders, and we don't blame people for epilepsy symptoms, we shouldn't blame people for ADHD symptoms either. But this analogy has revealing gaps.

Those who live with ADHD, as it happens, have an increased chance of having epilepsy, and I am an example of this co-morbidity. When I was a child, I had epilepsy, but it went away by the time I was four. I have no memory of it, and I had forgotten I'd ever had it by the time it hit me again in my late thirties, during the stress of buying a first house. My wife heard me collapse in the shower, and when I came to, I was standing in the hall, soaking wet, without a towel, gazing at her as she frantically tried to operate a telephone. She had run into the bathroom at the sound, discovered I was still breathing, tried and failed to rouse me, rushed to the telephone to call 911, and found she couldn't get her fingers to work. In the meantime, I had apparently walked out of the shower and down the hall, but I only regained consciousness as I was standing there. Fortunately, I had only one more seizure of this type before my doctor was able to prescribe medicine that controls my epilepsy.

This story probably seems rather extraordinary if you don't have epilepsy, because healthy non-epileptics have never experienced anything like this. But you have experienced the symptoms of both childhood and adult ADHD whether you have it or not: "Normal" kids call out in class, lose their math books, leave their seats, fidget, and find their mind wandering off their homework. "Normal" adults forget appointments, abandon projects without finishing them to start new projects, and ignore social cues because they get caught up in their own excitement. All of this is hallmark ADHD.

The difference between those properly diagnosed with ADHD and those without the disorder lies merely in the frequency of these symptoms. This does not disqualify ADHD from being a "real" disorder, but it does affect the way people respond to the symptoms. All of us, especially children, have occasional troubles with executive functions, so people who do not suffer from the disorder are tempted to view the symptoms of ADHD more as obstacles to be overcome, rather than unavoidable products of a disorder. It seems to them that if the attention disordered were to have trouble focusing or remembering, *they should just try harder, just like everyone else does.*

This idea never occurs to anyone in the case of seizures. People without epilepsy do not go through life trying not to have a seizure, so we would never even think to tell epileptics to try harder not to have seizures. (As a side note, a feeling of déjà vu precedes my seizures, which is common for epilepsy. When I experience déjà vu, I sometimes do in fact *try not* to have a seizure. But I don't think this "trying" really accomplishes anything, and I cannot even explain what I mean by such trying. Trying not to have a seizure is like trying to lift a cup off a table by the force of my mind—I can try, but I can't really explain what the trying consists of, and I have no confidence that it will work.)

In some ways, trying not to forget an appointment can be the same. This is how I sometimes remember an appointment: I am busy doing something, and suddenly, the idea of an approaching appointment pops into my head. If I fail, it is often because this happens after I've already missed my appointment. In this case, the idea of "trying harder" seems quite beside the point—since the idea just comes automatically, how am I supposed to bring my will to bear on it? Of course, there are ways: I could want the appointment so badly that I think of it constantly, or I could set a reminder on my phone (if I can remember to set the reminder, and if I pay close enough attention to set it correctly, and if I remember to have my phone nearby and the ringer set to audible.) I can do some of what everyone else does when they remember an appointment. Sometimes it even works.

One might argue that epilepsy, too, involves the will, because epileptics must choose to take their medicine, and remember to do so. But telling a person with ADHD to set an appointment reminder on their phone is different from telling an epileptic to remember to take medicine. Epilepsy does not affect one's ability to take medication, but ADHD makes it hard to remember to do things like setting a reminder. Living with ADHD, we often face the problem that the very things people recommend to us to "help us cope" with the disorder are themselves the sort of behavior that the disorder frustrates.

Frustrated by media stories questioning the reality of the disorder, Russell Barkley went so far as to organize an international statement testifying to scientific consensus on its reality, which you can view online at his website. We may hope that the spread of scientific knowledge will force the public to think of ADHD like they now think of epilepsy, but this seems unlikely. People never needed scientific knowledge of epilepsy to let go of the idea that seizures might represent lapses of will, because no one ever thought that seizures were lapses of will in the first place. Pre-scientific people attributed seizures to external causes like possession by gods or demons. When a person behaves in a way we don't even know *how* to behave ourselves, and that no one would want to behave, we tend to assume the behavior is involuntary. When someone behaves the same way we ourselves sometimes behave intentionally, we tend to attribute the behavior to intention. Claiming that ADHD is real does little to eradicate this inclination. In fact, people often accept completely that ADHD is real, then turn around and advise the afflicted to "just try harder" to overcome it. Those with epilepsy are never told to "just try harder" to overcome a seizure.

That is not all. Since ADHD symptoms all resemble commonplace behaviors of people without ADHD—varying in the disordered only with frequency—it seems logical to assume that the disordered must sometimes exhibit a bit of "regular" forgetfulness or impulsivity. With my ADD, I am more likely to forget appointments. Would I not do this occasionally even without my disorder? After all, people without the disorder forget appointments sometimes. Like me, they may be more likely to forget appointments they don't particularly want to keep. And nothing special marks my symptomatic appointment-forgetting as necessarily symptomatic. I forget appointments the same way everyone else does, as far as I can tell—*I just do it more often.* Assume I would forget X number of appointments without ADD. With the disorder, I forget X + Y number of appointments. Can I tell the X's from the Y's? I cannot, because instances of the disorder look and feel like non-disordered instances of the same unfortunate behavior. I can never know precisely, as I can with my epilepsy, whether *that was my disorder acting up*—or whether it was just *me* acting up. Barkley acknowledges that this is a problem for professionals dealing with ADHD sufferers when he writes about the vexation professionals feel working with those who are "unlikely, unable or unwilling" to perform. But those of us with the disorder face the same problem *from the inside.* Just because we exhibit the behavior doesn't mean we know whether to attribute it to a lapse of will or an incident of the disorder.

Unlike those with disorders such as epilepsy, those with ADHD cannot seem to avoid the question of the will:

Did I want to remember the appointment?

How badly did I want to remember?

Did I do everything I could to remember?

As soon as we accept the validity of any one of these questions, we welcome a complex set of problems. Westerners hold complicated beliefs about the will. We believe that we can muster greater or lesser quantities of will. We don't believe the outer limit of the will can be known and measured. We also believe that people can be mistaken about their own will. For all these reasons, it is always logically permissible, and usually sounds quite plausible, to say that someone might try harder at anything in which their intentions play a part.

This creates further problems with the analogy between ADHD and a disorder like epilepsy. The epileptic cannot bring on a seizure by force of will, nor can he will a seizure to stop. But it is possible for anyone, including the attention disordered, to forget, or talk too loudly, or allow their mind to wander, simply by not really intending to remember, remain quiet, or focus their mind. Indeed, any given ADHD-like behavior may either be the unwilled consequence of the disorder, or the expression of some sort of willful, weak, or self-deluding will. So we cannot attribute any specific instance of behavior solely to the disorder.

As it happens, researchers do not claim to be able to link any specific instance of behavior directly to the disorder. Barkley explains that though we have psychometric tests of executive function, these have been unreliable indicators of ADHD (*Executive Functions: What They Are, How They Work, and Why They Evolved* 9–13). ADHD is diagnosed by combining information from teachers, parents, and (less likely) mental health professionals who observe the subject in everyday functioning in home, school or work, and by ruling out other diagnoses (*Diagnostic and Statistical Manual of Mental Disorders: DSM-5* 61). In other words, the disorder is inferred by observing that certain behaviors, in themselves normal, occur in the subject with greater frequency than they do with other people. Such a diagnostic basis provides no grounds for determining that a specific instance of behavior is caused directly by the disorder. The most Barkley or other experts would say is that the disorder disposes a person to behave in certain likely ways—calling out, losing homework, wandering off task, fidgeting, getting out of seat, forgetting appointments, etc. Experts do not claim to know when, or if, the disorder prevents a subject from performing a specific task on a specific occasion.

If a researcher were able to monitor my son with some sort of device and inform his Spanish teacher that ADHD caused him to forget his homework on Tuesday and Wednesday, but he just did not try hard enough on Friday, the teacher would likely excuse his failure on Tuesday and Wednesday, but not on Friday. To do otherwise really would be like blaming an epileptic for his seizure. But no such device exists. In the next chapter we will see why constructing or even envisioning such a device raises what or probably insoluble questions about our concept of will, but for now, it is enough to know that researchers never claim to be able to separate a true instance of symptomatic behavior from a "regular" case of forgetting or impulsivity. They define ADHD as a disposition to behave in certain ways, and that is what they predict and describe when they use the label.

Unsurprisingly, teachers, parents, and others are reluctant to grant blanket amnesty for all ADD-like behavior merely because the attention disordered have a disposition to behave in certain ways. They wonder whether a mere disposition to behave in one way might be overcome by an exertion of the will in the opposite way. But we can't know whether or not that may be true for any specific instance. And it is the specific instances we are often asked to account for in our everyday lives.

I have no problem calling ADHD a disorder. But that doesn't solve our problem. We cannot declare that because a boy has ADHD, he did not mean to call out in class. A boy may have ADHD and also mean to call out in class. ADHD can be as "real" as we want, and still create a puzzle in the context of our concept of personal responsibility.

2 — Intentions Are Not Facts

My family has two dogs, and one of them is a black-and-white beagle who has earned a reputation as a ditz. She is unable to learn the game of fetch, for example. She eagerly races alongside our dachshund toward a tossed toy, but stands confused as the dachshund snatches it from the sky or ground and returns it. It is not that the dachshund gets there first: The beagle just doesn't get the concept of fetch, though she enjoys the general excitement of it. This beagle is pointlessly excited about everything, and perpetually happy. When I appear at our sliding glass door, she knows she must sit down before I will open it, but it takes her several minutes of jumping, running in circles, trying to sit, failing to sit, jumping, and running in a circle again before she can finally work off enough excitement to just sit.

So it makes for a stunning contrast when a siren sounds in the distance, and our ditzy beagle promptly sits and listens, with ears perked and head cocked. She then elongates her back, gazing up earnestly into the sky, and slowly, languorously, begins to howl. Our dachshund never joins in this solemn ritual, but the beagle observes it devoutly. As she does, I cannot help trying to make sense of her behavior by conjuring a scene: a pack of wild dogs arrayed across a mesa, a full moon, a hunt, a fallen dog, a threat, and a howl joined by each member of the pack. Our beagle's howl is sublime and noble. It invariably yields to comedy: As the siren fades away, and our beagle returns to normal, you can almost see a thought bubble form above her head as she asks herself, "What was all *that* about?"

A naturalist would reject my account as hopelessly anthropomorphized. I posit a personality—the silly "ditz"—and then project a romanticized view of the significance of howling onto my dog. I then conclude from these errors that she must share my bewilderment over her own behavior. For the naturalist, all behavior is just a combination of instinct and conditioning, and the idea that she would be puzzled when emerging from a howling episode is ridiculous. None of our dog's behavior could puzzle her, because it is merely instinctual, and a dog lacks the language to reflect on its own behavior.

One way to avoid the puzzle of this book—the puzzle of whether a disorder causes a behavior, or a person's own will causes a behavior—would be to follow the lead of the naturalist. We need merely to adopt the view that all human behavior, like dog behavior, is causally determined. In this view, people may still have a will, but causal forces determine the strength and direction of that will. Just as the naturalist explains dog behavior as a result of instinct and conditioning, researchers explain human behavior as causal matters of genotype, phenotype, conditioning and socialization.

Adopting this scientific, deterministic view of human behavior drains the moral force from our puzzle. When we withhold blame from an individual for behavior caused by a disorder, we do so because we think the disorder determines his behavior, so he cannot help but do what he does. As soon as we accept the deterministic view, it would seem that no one—disordered or not— could help doing anything he or she does. My beagle cannot do anything other than what she does when she howls; I cannot do anything other than forget appointments when I forget them; and you cannot do anything other than remember appointments when you remember them. Everybody, in this view, merely does what they do because of what they are when they do it. In this view, people with disorders like ADHD are not unique for being unable to help what they do. If it is causally determined that those with a low capacity for self-control will be undisciplined, it is also causally determined that those with excellent self-control will behave with discipline. This is precisely the view Russell Barkley takes in *ADHD and the Nature of Self-Control* (319). Behavior will differ between those with or without disorders, in this view, but all behavior— disordered or not—shares the same status of being determined solely by a causal matrix. What reason would we have to hold people morally responsible for what they do? Adopting a causal determinist worldview neatly solves the problem of responsibility that this book is trying to address.

This determinist view has firm support within the field of psychology. Both Sigmund Freud, the father of psychoanalysis, and B. F. Skinner, the famous proponent of behaviorism, were determinists. Of the seven schools of contemporary psychology—behavioral, psychoanalytic, humanistic, cognitive, evolutionary, biological, and sociocultural—only the humanistic school tries to understand human behavior as an expression of free will. Barkley explains that while those with ADHD struggle to direct their behavior toward goals across time, the typical person, who can fluently direct behavior across time, is not free; he is merely governed by the promise of future reward as well as present reward.

"Our will, therefore, is not free" (*ADHD and the Nature of Self-Control* 205).

Behavioral scientists have good reason to adopt this view, because they seek to explain and predict human behavior. If behavior is determined causally, it can be explained and predicted. If individuals produce behavior through some autonomous, indeterminate, uncaused, or "free" process, how could it be explained or predicted? A scientist who held open the possibility of some sort of spontaneous, uncaused source of behavior could never rule out that possibility. Studies would routinely have to conclude with an equivocation: Either identified causal matrix X caused behavior A, or else subjects just chose to exhibit behavior A all on their own as an expression of their free will.

As much as behavioral scientists value the causal model of behavior, few people want to apply it to their actual lives. Faced with choices, we often believe we can choose to go one way or another, and that the outcome depends on some special, essentially human capacity we have to freely choose. We certainly accept the influence of genetic, physical, and environmental forces on our lives, but we still want to believe that after these forces are accounted for, we remain free to choose at least some of our actions.

Advocates for the attention disordered understand the popularity of the idea of free will, so when they urge accommodations, they seldom argue, as a true determinist would, that people with ADHD are merely acting out their set of determining causal forces, just like the rest of us act out ours. Instead, they argue that those with ADHD have a disorder that prevents them from controlling their own behavior, and thereby draw an implicit contrast between the disordered and those without disorders, who *can freely* control *their* behavior. Advocates seldom claim that people should not be held morally responsible for behavior, instead, they insist that the presence of a disorder should excuse the attention disordered.

The implication is that the disorder interferes with an otherwise free will. Saying that our free will can be compromised by a disorder is a convenient and much more socially palatable alternative to making the controversial claim that no one has free will. The downside is that this approach creates the puzzle this book addresses: When, exactly, are the attention disordered displaying a symptom, and when are they acting on their own free will?

I don't wish to take a position on whether we should reject the concept of free will. I merely want to highlight the fact that when we discard the complete determinism of science in favor of the more popular view that a disorder is an outside force that acts against an otherwise free will, we introduce a puzzle into the lives of the disordered.

If the puzzle bothers us, we have a way to make it seem reasonable. The key is to imagine a future science that will sort it all out for us. In the future, we tell ourselves, science will be able to distinguish purely symptomatic behavior from seemingly identical behavior that should actually be charged to a weak or self-deceptive will. For now, we must guess, but only because we lack the science. This formulation conserves a very attractive set of beliefs: belief in the power of science, in the innocence of the disordered, and in the viability of the concept of free will. It also kicks a very troublesome can a long way down the road. Does the belief that science can one day sort out this puzzle make sense?

Suppose a researcher wants to determine not merely that a subject has ADHD, but that the disorder alone caused a specific instance of his behavior. She would need to rule out alternate possibilities; for example, that the subject did not truly intend to avoid exhibiting the behavior in question. We cannot rely on him to report his own true intentions, because he may not know his own intentions. A common feature of our idea of intention includes the notion that we can be mistaken about our own true intentions, such as when we harbor subconscious intentions, or indulge in self-deception. So the researcher would need to know his true intention and not merely rely on his self-report about it. She would need to know his intention as a matter of *fact*.

The Holden Caulfield Thought Experiment

I would like to pose what philosophers call a "thought experiment" to demonstrate the difficulty a scientist would face in trying to establish an intention as a fact. To do this, my experiment involves comparing the relationship of fact to intention in literature to the same relationship in real life, by examining a scene from J. D. Salinger's novel *Catcher in the Rye*. I do not claim that the main character, Holden Caulfield, has ADHD. I just choose the book because it seemed to speak directly to me during my most troubled times as a teenager, and I suspect it has appealed to others with the disorder as well. Like us, Holden struggles to find his place in the world.

In the opening scene, Holden exhibits behavior which makes us wonder about his intentions. Before examining that troubling case of intention, let's look at simpler problems of fact in the novel.

Though a novel is a fictional world, this doesn't prevent us from delineating certain facts within it. It is a fact, for example, that Holden Caulfield's family is moneyed. Holden's father works as a corporate lawyer, he invests in plays on Broadway, and sends Holden to a series of expensive prep schools. In one of these schools, Holden's Mark Cross suitcases intimidate his roommate. Does Holden's family have money? Fiction or not, this is a factual question with a factual answer: yes.

There are other questions in the novel for which no factual answer can be found. The reader does not know if Holden was delivered by Caesarean section. Holden declares in the first sentence of the book that he's not going to tell us anything personal about his parents, and he doesn't offer any details of his birth. This fact isn't in the novel, and our conventions of novel-reading provide nowhere else to look for it.

Suppose Holden were a real person, though, as opposed to a fictional character. In that case, the facts of his birth would exist at some time and place in the world. Everybody is born somehow. Even if we didn't know the answer, there would have to be an answer. A novel offers a limited set of (make-believe) facts, while the real world contains *all* the facts.

Now, let us attempt this Fictional Holden/Real Holden experiment with a question of intention.

Early in the novel, we learn Holden has lost some fencing equipment in the NYC subway. This proves disastrous, because his team ends up forfeiting their match because of it. Holden says it was an accident. He doesn't seem to have ditched the equipment intentionally—he didn't hide it from the team, for example—but he may not have formed a serious enough intention to safeguard it. He may have thought he wanted to keep hold of the equipment, but his intention in this regard may well have been weak or self-deceptive.

The book offers plenty of facts that bear on this question. Holden was the manager of Pencey Prep's fencing team. Holden was in charge of the equipment. Holden left the equipment on the subway. And according to Holden, the whole team ostracized him on the way home. So the team, at least, holds him responsible. In their minds, Holden did not take his duty seriously enough to accomplish it.

Against their view, we might maintain that Holden just made a natural mistake in a difficult situation. He had nothing to gain by forgetting the equipment. He says he had to keep getting up to check the subway schedule to figure out where they were supposed to get off, so he was distracted. He may have gotten up to check the schedule, suddenly realized that this was their stop, and called to the team to get off. In the moment the train doors opened he was preoccupied with getting the team off the subway, so he forgot the equipment. Had the timing of these variables worked out differently, he may well have had a moment to return to his seat and remember the equipment, but it didn't work out that way. It was an accident, and not a product of his intention.

On the other hand, Holden isolates himself from others throughout the book. He seldom commits himself unreservedly to any shared endeavor with the people around him, virtually all of whom he judges to be phonies. He may not have cared about the team enough to remember their equipment. He may have resented them for their enthusiasm and sense of belonging, and neglected their equipment subconsciously out of spite. This contention gains support from his reaction to his mistake: He feels sorry for himself because the team ostracizes him. A team manager who truly cared about his team might be more saddened by the ruined match than miffed about their treatment of him. In his final verdict on the situation, he tells the reader, "It was pretty funny, in a way." These do not sound like the words of a young man who truly regrets his error. It seems Holden never really cared much about his teammates or the equipment, and it was never truly his intention to protect it.

Yet many readers may still hesitate to blame Holden. Holden is troubled. He had just been kicked out of Pencey Prep when he lost the equipment. His expulsion becomes the catalyst for the psychological breakdown the book chronicles, and which eventually lands him in psychiatric care. He may not have been able, at this point in his life, to handle a complicated and stressful situation. In this view, his dismissal of the event as funny, which on the surface seems so damning, might be interpreted as a defensive reaction, rather than a blatant expression of contempt. He intended to perform his duty, but he just wasn't up to it, and he protects himself from the full impact of his failure by adopting an ironic distance.

This dispute could continue for as long as anybody would like to contribute to it, but it should be clear by now that no one fact or set of facts would emerge as the fact of Holden's intention. Instead, the facts contribute to an *interpretation*, which seems to be all we are going to get. The field is not completely open—an interpretation that misstated or ignored facts would not persuade us—but there is certainly space for more than one interpretation. This is no surprise, for this is exactly the kind of thing we enjoy in a novel.

Let us now return to the real world, as we did when we wondered if Holden was delivered by C-section. The real world would have to contain, in some time and place, the fact of Holden's birth. Would it also have to hold the fact of his intention? We can certainly find more facts about Real Holden than we can about Fictional Holden. We could examine Real Holden's interactions with his team on other occasions. We could replay security camera tape from the subway. We could learn whether or not he had a history of forgetting things. We could hear how his teammates viewed his conduct in their own words, rather than just relying on his account. We could examine the notes of his psychiatrist, and subject Real Holden to a battery of neurological and psychiatric tests.

Yet none of this would do more than return us to our original problem. No additional fact could stand as the fact of Holden's intention. More facts might shift the argument, perhaps persuasively, but a *persuasive interpretation* is not the same thing as a *fact*. Suppose we had a mythical lie detector with an error rate of zero. We could ask Holden how seriously he intended to safeguard the fencing equipment—but what could he tell us? Depending on his mood and on how we phrased the question, we could get different answers from Holden at different times. Holden is uncertain about his own intentions. But even if he assured us he was confident in his statement, and we asked him how he knew that, what would he say then? He would have nothing to offer us but an interpretation.

Intentions do not manifest themselves like perceptions or sensations, simply appearing directly to our consciousness, like the sight of an orange lawn chair or a feeling of nausea. Instead, we identify our own intentions the same way we identify other people's intentions—by a process of interpretation. If the lie detector worked, and if Holden said he felt sure he meant to safeguard the fencing equipment, the only fact we could honestly report is that Holden interprets his intention as benign. In our use of the word intention, people can be wrong about their intentions—so why couldn't Holden be wrong about his? We accept no final word when an intention is under dispute. Intention is a matter of interpretation, not a matter of fact.

With the outcome of this thought experiment in mind, we can return to our original problem. We had wondered if science could someday tell us what we truly intend, so we could distinguish failures of will or instances of self-deception from behavior caused by a disorder. Could it tell me, for example, whether I forgot an appointment because of my ADD or because I never truly intended to go? Our hope was to arrest the endless go-around that such questions engender by finding a terminal fact. If science could offer such facts, we could stop guessing about it. In theory, at least, with a sufficiently mobile testing kit, my son's teacher would know whether to offer him specific accommodations at particular moments. I would know whether or not to blame my son when he forgets to bring his math book home. My wife would know whether I'm doing my best to attend to her feelings when she expresses them, and I would know, too.

What this thought experiment reveals is that we are wrong if we imagine we are doing the best we can with a limited science. Our notion of intention does not comport itself with science. It requires a literary style of interpretation. We do not interpret intentions as some sort of stopgap measure while we wait for a science that would establish intentions as facts. We interpret intentions because, for us, an intention is not a fact at all, but a conclusion reached by interpretation. We construct the intentions of people in real life—even our own —through the same process of interpretation we use in literature. When all the facts are in, they do not reveal a factual answer to the question of intention. The facts merely form a field of literary play. The interpretation of intention has no necessary end-point. We can always start interpreting again, and perhaps reach a different conclusion. As soon as we begin to wonder if we were *unable* to perform, or just *unwilling*, we have broken loose into a field of literary interpretation. We may satisfy ourselves with one conclusion or another, but no conclusion will have the stolid, inflexible determinacy of fact.

The idea that science will establish the fact of our intentions does not rest on over-confidence in science; it hinges on a distortion of our use of the word "intention." It is as misguided to imagine a science that could tell us the truth of our intentions as it would be to try to invent one that could tell us whether Holden Caulfield truly meant to safeguard the foils.

The good news is that when we let go of the idea that science will someday solve the puzzle for us, we open a surprising door to resolving it ourselves today.

3 — Resentment, Gratitude, and ADHD

When I was six, according to my memory of the event, my mother told me that my new stepfather was a "mountain climber." If she actually said this, it was a bit of an exaggeration. When I discovered he wouldn't even go car camping, I joined the Boy Scouts. I enjoyed many hikes and campouts. Once, though, I went hiking, not with my usual troop, but with an inter-troop group of boys trying to get enough hikes in for a merit badge. The adult in charge of this group was incompetent, and after we made the summit, he steered us off the trail and down a ravine. Worse, he neglected to put an adult at the front of our group. So I joined up with a Scout from my troop named David, who was a year younger than me and the son of our Scoutmaster, and we sailed out in front of the group, virtually skating down a rocky slope. Thinking back on our descent, I remember singing and feeling elated. Later, I would learn to identify that sort of elation as a symptom of my disorder, and when I became aware of it, I would quite consciously rein it in. On this occasion, I may have sobered just a little when the slope flattened out onto a rock shelf; David and I stood, looking down at a cliff dropping away below us.

We looked around, and saw no way to bypass the cliff. It was either turn around and hike all the way back to the summit, or descend the cliff. We had never descended a cliff on a hike before, and it seemed obvious that even if we did, the Scouts behind us would not follow us, but I announced that I would climb down the cliff. When I got to the bottom, I explained, maybe I could look back up and find another route down that everyone could take. I positioned myself over a groove in the course rock, turned around to face the rock, planted my boot in the V-shaped groove, and began to descend, looking down between my legs to position my feet, and using handholds in the rock in front of me.

When I was about ten feet down, David called down after me, asking if it was easy. I shouted back that it was, and continued climbing down, hearing the sound of David placing his own boots in the groove. After descending ten more feet, I saw what looked to me like a burlap sack fluttering past me. It was David, and he would fall another ten or fifteen feet to land with a thud at the foot of the cliff, blocked from my view by the curve of the rock face.

I accelerated my descent in terror until I could survey the ground directly at the foot of the cliff. I still could not see David. At this point the rock face had gone from nearly vertical to actually receding into a negative pitch. Only if I had some preternatural ability to hold the rock with my hands while my feet dangled free could I climb down this section. I sized up the remaining drop, and decided I could probably just lower myself a little further and then let myself fall without injury. I did so, landed on the rocky debris at the bottom of the cliff, and lifted up my head. I saw David, sprawled on his back among some rocks, alive, but his face covered in blood.

The rest of the day I spent tending more or less ineffectually to David. A two-inch-long triangle of flesh had been scooped out from his head, revealing his skull, and I placed a piece of gauze over it. I tied twigs to a wrist that was wildly out of joint. I fell into self-protective, shock-induced naps, interrupted at times by David's cries as he heard rocks bouncing down the cliff. The other Scouts had assembled above the cliff, and they were busy goofing around and blithely knocking rocks down on us, so I would have to jump up at intervals to hunch over David and protect him from the falling rocks. The Scout leader came down with the help of a rope, and then continued down the ravine, going for help. At dusk a helicopter arrived, lowering county search-and-rescue guys who strapped David to a stretcher and whisked him back up with one of the rescuers. The wind had kicked up, hampering helicopter maneuvers, so the remaining rescue guy asked me if I thought I could climb back up the cliff with his help. I said I would. Climbing up was much easier than climbing down, and after rejoining the other Scouts, we hiked all the way back out of the ravine, meeting volunteers at the top with flashlights and hot cocoa, and they hiked us all the way back down.

David's father, my Scoutmaster, called me the next day to tell me David would be okay. He didn't have brain damage, and his two broken wrists would heal. I was afraid the father would blame me for stupidly leading his son down the cliff, but instead he praised me for taking care of him and sheltering him from the falling rocks. He called me a hero. I had always wanted to be a hero, but I couldn't help feeling privately that I was to blame. After this, I would alternate proud memories of my heroism with guilty, and momentary, acceptance of my foolhardiness. When I thought about my elation on the scree slope, and the naked rationalization I engaged in to justify my choice to climb down the cliff, I felt the bottom drop out of my sense of self, and I worked to replace those thoughts with other thoughts.

Eventually, though, I began to associate my behavior in the ravine before the fall with my ADD, with the fall transmuting into a kind of lurking terror in my mind, a warning of what might happen in the future if I did not exercise a constant vigilance against the vagaries of my disordered brain. At the same time, I wondered if I wasn't deceiving myself by blaming my behavior on my disorder, just as I'd deceived myself before, wallowing in easy fantasies of heroism. I hadn't simply jumped from scree slope to cliff, without thinking. I thought it through quite seriously, even to the point of rationalizing the decision I already knew I wanted to make. Can I really count the deliberate rationalization of a poor decision as an instance of ADD? My rationalization wasn't exactly impulsive. If anything, it was goal-directed: I wanted to climb down the cliff, so I invented a rationale, and avoided the consideration of counter-arguments. The flaw in my thinking might be better viewed not as an example of impulsivity but of self-deception. Was I disordered at the top of the cliff, or dishonest?

Once again we are worrying about Holden Caulfield's lost foils, with higher moral stakes. The high moral stakes are an anomaly. Usually, those with ADHD worry about a lost homework assignment, a missed appointment, an injudicious outburst or comment, or a forgotten set of keys. These problems seldom rise to a level that could provoke moral condemnation. Still, even these minor problems have always compelled me to wonder if my mistakes represent a conquest of my will by a disorder, or the sly impositions of a flawed or troublesome will.

A key contribution to the free will debate by a philosopher named Peter Strawson helped me link the evident moral issues involved in leading a younger boy off a cliff to small errors of slight moral dimension. His work reveals how the concept of free will is intrinsic to many human actions that carry only marginal moral stakes. Only with his insights can we gain an adequate understanding of the way this issue impacts the lives of the attention disordered.

Strawson is not concerned with dilemmas faced by the disordered, but by the philosophical argument called incompatibilism, which states that free will is incompatible with determinism. He wants to show that even if free will were judged by philosophers to be incompatible with determinism, we would have little choice but to retain our belief in free will. He does this by arguing that the concept of free will is indispensable, because it forms the foundation not just for moral censure, but for feelings of resentment and gratitude, as well as pride and guilt. Without a notion of free will, we could not make sense of these emotions. Since Strawson doesn't think we can stop feeling these feelings and still recognize ourselves as the people we are, he cannot envision a future without the concept of free will (see his essay reprinted in Watson, 72–93). I am not concerned here with arguments about the compatibility of free will and determinism, but Strawson's argument creates an invaluable byproduct: It illuminates the true dimensions of living with the puzzle of ADHD.

Strawson explains the concept of resentment by sketching a scenario in which a man steps on another man's hand. Strawson asserts that the man whose hand is stepped upon is going to feel pain. If the man trod upon the victim's hand on purpose, the victim will still feel pain, but according to Strawson, he will also feel something else: resentment.

Strawson's point is that resentment is distinguished from anger only by an attribution of intention. We would not need the word resentment if we lacked any belief in free will, because the word anger would suffice to capture everything we could claim any reason to feel. We would have no justification for claiming to feel something special when we think someone harmed us on purpose. Believing in free will, we feel something special when we think someone meant to do us harm. Without some idea of free will, what would be so special about *meaning to do* something? In such a world, we could still become angry with each other—in the same way that we become angry at a missed putt, a broken fingernail, or a car that won't start—but we would no longer have any use for the word "resentment"; this is because without any notion that the will is free, we could no longer comprehend the nuance that the word "resentment" captures.

We would also no longer need the concept of gratitude. If I run out of water on a hike, become thirsty, and someone tosses me a canteen full of water, I will feel grateful to that person. If I discover this person was unconcerned with my thirst, but only meant to lighten his own load, I will still be pleased to have the water, but I will lack any justification for gratitude. Gratitude is properly reserved for people who actually intend to do us good. Being grateful to someone implies that they have a free will.

Strawson suggests the term "reactive attitudes" to describe those attitudes that depend upon a belief in free will. He fills out this category by adding moral condemnation and moral praise, ingeniously suggesting that they are vicarious forms of resentment and gratitude. When we condemn a thief for his crime, we are expressing resentment on behalf of the thief's victims. When we praise the firefighter who rescues a man from a conflagration, in Strawson's view this is a form of vicarious participation in the rescued man's gratitude. This also explains our reactive attitudes toward offenses that have no direct victim. When faced with an otherwise harmless act that he deems offensive, a religious man may condemn it in the name of God; he joins the Creator in vicarious resentment. Similarly, an environmentalist of the sentimental variety may condemn polluters on behalf of a resentful Nature, or a humanist may deplore a charismatic demagogue on behalf of truth.

Just as Strawson analogizes resentment up into higher and more abstract domains of moral sentiment, we may extrapolate down to the attitudes of guilt and pride. We can view these feelings as internalized, self-regarding forms of resentment and gratitude. It seems plausible to suppose that we learn guilt and pride from the resentful or grateful behavior of our primary caregivers. When we feel guilt, it is like resenting oneself, and pride represents a feeling of gratitude for oneself. When David's father chose not to blame me for my behavior at the top of the cliff, it was a great relief to me, but it did not negate my guilt. I already had a sort of internalized father inside me, and I could not evade his pointing finger.

The first time I read Strawson's account, I experienced a revelation about my disorder. I had always been aware that I faced moral accusations for my ADD-behavior, and I knew they gave me a feeling of puzzlement, because I often didn't feel truly responsible for what I'd done. But formal accusations of moral blame are actually quite rare, and often my accusers shared my confusion about whether or not I was truly guilty. So why did the issue of moral blame loom so large? By linking free will to a constellation of reactive attitudes, Strawson reveals the true scope of the problem. I am not only puzzled by moral blame, but by resentment. Resentment is pervasive in the lives of the attention disordered, and often perceptible even when unspoken. Strawson's insight helped me discover the unseen power of resentment in my life and those of others with ADD.

Even more insidiously, when we avoid manifesting our symptoms, we often receive the gratitude of others who are happily surprised that for once, we didn't screw up. Like resentment, gratitude carries the message that we intended our action. This only sets us up for resentment when our symptoms return. In accepting the gratitude of those who are pleased that we managed to suppress our symptoms, we accept along with it the covert claim that symptomatic behavior is actually governed by intent. Shame and pride, no less than resentment and gratitude, occasion this same confusion, suffered in the isolation of our own minds. This is why we cannot feel ashamed or proud without also feeling confused and apprehensive.

In cataloging the attitudes that assume a free will on the part of the actor—resentment, gratitude, guilt, and pride—Strawson inadvertently identifies attitudes that are both puzzling and poisonous for the attention disordered. We have already discovered that we will never know, in the case of apparently symptomatic behavior, whether these attitudes are warranted or not. But while these reactive attitudes may be a necessary part of human behavior generally, we are not required to display them as responses to all behavior—nor are they the only means we have to discourage unwanted behavior. The obvious solution is to devise means to avoid displaying these attitudes in responding to apparently symptomatic behavior. In the next chapter I will build on this insight, showing how reactive attitudes adversely affect the child with ADHD, and begin to develop a framework for mitigating such reactivity in the context of disordered behavior.

4 — How Reactivity Shapes the Child

As a young boy, I once met a friend outside my family's suburban California house. He needed a place to lock up his bicycle. I looked around and spotted a row of lawn sprinkler valves, took a step toward them, and gave them an appraising kick. My friend decided to just leave the bicycle in the garage. I went around and opened the garage.

Later that day, when my friend went home, I heard a knock on the door to my room. It was my stepfather.

"Scott," he asked, "Did you do anything with the sprinkler valves?"

"No," I responded.

"I'd like you to come see something."

I followed him outside and saw our front driveway four inches deep in water. Now that I thought about it, I said, I *had* given the sprinkler valve a little kick to see if it might be a good place to lock up my friend's bicycle.

"Why would you do that?" my stepfather asked. And as soon as he asked, I realized there could be no logical answer. What would the kick accomplish, other than, say, breaking the valve? If the kick was a test for weakness, how would that weakness manifest itself, other than in an outright failure? The act made no sense.

"I don't know," I said.

"I don't want to punish you, Scott. I really . . . I just want to know one thing," he said. "What was going on in your head?"

"I don't know," I said.

What was going on in your head? This question, depending on how it is asked, may be an accusation, or it may come from a place of innocent inquiry. Like overt resentment, this question attributes intention. It assumes that thought processes that may be automatic and non-conscious are available to introspection. If ADHD is a breakdown of non-conscious systems of self-regulation failed, how would I experience this consciously? I didn't know what was going on in my head. Searching my mind for the moment when I would have thought about the consequences of my actions, I found a void. Was the void my fault? By asking this question, my stepfather was trying to step away from assigning blame, of punishing, of resenting, but he didn't know how to step out far enough. The very question he asked in an attempt at empathy was a sharp jab at the most puzzled and sensitive area of my self-consciousness.

What we want to do, as parents, is avoid such reactivity. We want to avoid attributing intention to the behavior characteristic of ADHD. The issue of reactivity is just as important for the adult, but to understand reactivity as an adult we need to first see how it was learned in childhood. It is in childhood that we can most easily picture its consequences. Our childhood experience is with us still.

The Dance of Intersubjectivity

When my stepfather asked me if I'd touched the sprinkler valves, I first tried to lie, and then reverted to the truth. All of us recognize these as the usual child options. If a child tells the truth, he may endure an interval of coldness, anger, or reproach from his parent. Since a young child depends on the parent for everything, this can be disturbing. But the parent may indicate a path toward reconciliation: The child can simply apologize. To perform an apology properly, he should recall his moment of culpability—the moment when, facing two choices, he chose the bad one. Of this, he must repent. This will gain him reconciliation with the parent, but also something else: He will recognize that he has an inner experience others can guess at, because they have inner experiences, too. The experience of transgression and apology is a key experience that fosters a belief in *intersubjectivity*, or the concept that other people have an inner life—a subjective experience—that is like one's own. We cannot observe another person's subjectivity. We cannot experience the world from inside someone else's mind. One way we come to believe that others have inner worlds, just like we do, is watching other people make guesses about our own inner world that accord with our own experience of this world. One key form this takes is when people try to attribute intentions to us.

If a child chooses to lie to cover up his misdeed, he may—if the parent accepts his lie—avoid scolding or punishment. But he will miss an opportunity to develop his sense of intersubjectivity. This is one reason parents fear deceit. Deceit not only masks off an area of the child's subjectivity from the parent, it also prevents the child from developing a sense that others have an inner world like his own.

When both parent and child agree that the child felt an urge to do something, and he knew it was wrong, but acted on it anyway, this forms a powerful moment of intersubjectivity. If the child denies what he knows to be true, he replaces intersubjectivity with distrust. Rather than experiencing reconciliation and redemption, which offers the possibility of recognizing the parent's inner feelings along with his own, the child who lies learns to see other people as externalities subject to his manipulation. Although there will be other chances for this child to come to believe in the subjectivities of others, the practice of lying impedes the growth of intersubjectivity.

How ADHD Confuses Attribution and Impedes Intersubjectivity

If this model is valid, it has unfortunate implications for the attention disordered. Lying is not one of our symptoms, though our disorder gives us plenty of occasions to lie. But even when we don't lie, we miss out on moments of intersubjectivity, much as the liar does, because disordered behavior is such a poor candidate for intersubjectivity. Our experience of transgression is not the sort of experience one can easily repent of, because we aren't sure we did anything wrong. I wasn't thinking about anything much when I kicked the sprinkler valve. Had I kicked the sprinkler valve to show off in front of my friend, I could have soundly repented. My stepfather would not need to have asked me what had been going on in my head, because he could have guessed based on his own experience of misbehaving as a young boy.

But as it was, even with my confession, my stepfather could not recognize what it was like to be me. My stepfather was caught in the puzzle of ADD; he guessed that I hadn't meant anything by my action, and didn't know, in that case, what he was supposed to make of it. I did not think I had had a malign intent, so I felt confused about my own guilt. Since he didn't punish me, I understood that I should feel grateful toward him. But when he appeared dumbfounded by my behavior, and asked me "what was going on in my head," I felt like an alien. I was judged to be a person with an incomprehensible brain. Rather than feeling grateful, I felt resentful toward him for pointing out how strange I was, and then I felt guilty for that.

Suppose, instead, that my stepfather had asked me to apologize. An honest ADD child who is asked to apologize has two options, and each has implications for his development.

As an agreeable child, I could have apologized, even though I had no memory of any malign intent, and could not picture myself having acted differently than

I did. This would validate my stepfather's attribution of my intention, at the cost of suppressing my own internal attribution. Doing this over the long term would seem likely to inculcate a tendency to doubt my own attributions and distrust my own intentions.

Had I been a willful child, I might have rejected blame for the decision. I might have denied any intention in the matter, and insisted that because I hadn't intended to break the sprinkler, I should not have to apologize for kicking it. A parent is likely to reject such a claim, and feel resentful of the child who sticks to it. A long-term commitment to this strategy would seem likely to cause me to distrust other people. I might come to view others as ill-intentioned and hostile, because they persist in assigning me blame for behavior that I regard as blameless.

I have experienced both of these processes as a person with ADHD, and seen both of them in my son's life. Both of us can vacillate between a forlorn feeling that we are worthless and to blame for everything, and a prickly and brittle sense that we are victims of injustice. I am happy to say that I am far less susceptible to these attitudes now than I was as a young person, and my son has never been as susceptible to them as I was. I would attribute my own success to years of therapy, and I'd like to think my son has benefitted from the approach I am explaining in this book.

In addition to the primary responses of simple acceptance or rejection of the attribution, logic suggests two possible secondary responses. The gap between the child's own attribution of intention and that of others may create cognitive dissonance, which is the psychologist's word for the anxiety we feel when we try to hold two opposing thoughts together in our minds. If the cognitive dissonance becomes intolerable, the child has a perverse remedy that will bring inner and outer attributions into harmony: He can misbehave willfully. If he willfully misbehaves, his internal attribution of guilt will, for once, agree with others' attributions. He may be punished for his misbehavior, of course, but his cognitive dissonance will be erased and he will gain the experience of intersubjectivity. Those who blame him will be right! It may be easier to simply become the bad child you are accused of being than to endure a persistent gap in attribution.

As it happens, experts in ADHD routinely counsel parents and teachers to watch for "self-fulfilling prophesies" or "downward spirals of negativity" that can drag down the attention-disordered child from merely exhibiting symptomatic behavior to willful and demonstrative acting out. I believe these warnings are ways of naming and explaining the behavior my model hypothesizes. If I'm right, children with ADHD may develop secondary symptoms of willfulness and defiance as a way to bring inner and outer attributions of intention into alignment.

Responding to Blame for Apparently Symptomatic Behavior	
Individual response	**Long-term outcome for individual**
Accepts blame	Cognitive dissonance, distrusts self
Rejects blame	Cognitive dissonance, distrusts others
Acts out intentionally	Cognitive assonance, maladaptive
Proclaims own subjectivity while rejecting others' views	Cognitive assonance, adaptive, alienated worldview
Asserts own subjectivity while accepting others' views	Cognitive assonance, adaptive, harmonized worldview

The logical space of the model suggests another option. Though it seems problematic that inner and outer attributions of intentions cannot be made to agree on so many occasions, this is only problematic if one believes that they must or should agree. A maturing teen or young adult may develop a worldview that denies this claim, which would allow her to avoid the ongoing cognitive dissonance of trying to resolve conflicting attributions. She could come to believe that she holds her own truth about her subjective experience, which others cannot understand and which they are often wrong about. She would then reject others' attributions about her behavior, and insist that they cannot know how she feels. This behavior would represent the kind of worldview that holds that each of us is fundamentally alone, trapped inside our own subjectivity and unable to reach beyond it to understand the world in which others live. This is the view of the archetypal "alienated" teen and of popular existentialism—and it was my own experience in my teen years.

I believe this dark view has a positive counterpart. Some may become agnostic about attributions, and accept that oneself and another may make conflicting attributions without supposing this to be a crisis. In other words, one may decide that others' attributions need not match her own, without believing that this means that she is alone. She could assert her own subjective stance, while accepting that others are free to form their own views independently, and let go of the insistence that these views must either match her own or be judged as incorrect.

The last possibility offers the most appealing option for those with ADHD. To live it, we need to be able to avoid conflict with others about our intentions. Others may still very much expect us to agree with their attributions of intention, so we need a way to cope with their demands that doesn't involve trying to persuade them to adopt our own attributions. This requires learning how to strip away the attributions inherent in reactive attitudes like resentment and gratitude. Existing psychological literature already offers a practical method for doing this, but to understand its value to us we need to first take a closer look at the difference between reactivity and non-reactivity, and look at the whole issue in the context of parenting, which is where we each learned our own distinctive way of coping with attributions.

5 — Infractions Versus Crimes: Understanding Reactivity

Suppose a man lives in a big city and drives a car. This man hates carrying change and messing around with parking meters, but his favorite parking spots are metered. He parks without feeding the meters, and pays the fines later. He regards parking tickets as a business expense.

Although his approach seems extravagant, the law condones this behavior on some level. Parking violations are infractions, not crimes. The vast majority of infractions do not require the law to make any finding of intent, so it does not matter whether the man is committing parking violations intentionally or not. The law has no interest in his intent, and issues no moral judgment. Whether someone forgets to pay the meter, decides not to pay the meter, or decides to render CPR to a person in need rather than feeding the meter, the law responds in the same way. It issues a fine.

With most crimes, though, the law very much concerns itself with intent. A criminal conviction typically *requires* a finding of intent. If I walk out of a store hiding a DVD under my jacket to avoid paying, the law must find me guilty of theft. If someone places a DVD in my backpack without my knowledge, and I walk out unknowingly, I should not be convicted. Some crimes even offer a spectrum of intent. If I hit and kill a pedestrian with my car, the law has a range of options. The death may be ruled accidental, or a case of negligent manslaughter, or reckless manslaughter, or even murder. The difference hinges entirely on a finding about my intentions.

To put it another way, the law takes a non-reactive stance toward parking behavior. The law assigns no moral blame and displays no interest in intent. If the motorist pays his fines promptly, he never needs to face so much as a scolding. The law does not resent the rich man who regards his fines as a cost of business. Perhaps his community may want to look at the fines and make sure they fairly reflect the cost to the community of the lost parking space; if not, they might want to raise the fines. But the community would struggle to find legal expression for any resentment they feel toward this man, because for this particular action, the law assigns no *moral* responsibility. The responsibility for such an infraction is not moral; it is pecuniary.

But for a crime like murder, the law demands a finding of intent, and the concomitant moral blame. Were a murderer to take the same approach as the rich man takes to parking, the law—and society—would not be content to watch him murder, serve his time, and murder again. The time served cannot begin to make us whole for the harm a murderer has done. We feel compelled to exact repayment in moral coin, which is why the law examines prior convictions and looks for remorse at sentencing and prior to parole.

Non-Reactive Consequences

I suggest that we shape our responses to symptom-like behaviors on the model of the parking ticket and not, as is otherwise common, the criminal conviction. Our responses to symptom-like behaviors should avoid any attribution of intent. This is not because the person with ADHD is necessarily innocent of malign intention, but because neither we nor the disordered person can really come to know their intention, so it is everyone's advantage to avoid making an attribution. We need a set of non-reactive consequences, responses that—like parking tickets—imply no moral responsibility. Non-reactive consequences will avoid triggering the problems with attribution and intersubjectivity we have explored, because they do not prompt any puzzles about the will.

While the analogy of infractions versus crimes nicely illustrates an important distinction, there are two important caveats. One is that this analogy tends to focus our attention on negative consequences, but positive consequences are actually more powerful. But positive consequences, as we have seen in the case of gratitude, are just as likely to be reactive, so the principle is the same.

The other concern involves a potential confusion. Because infractions are generally less severely punished than crimes, the suggestion that we give parking tickets rather than jail terms can be misunderstood as a plea for leniency. It is important that we see the flaw in this way of thinking, because many people respond to the vexing problem of ADHD with leniency. Leniency by itself, though, is of no use. Being lenient does nothing to help us avoid attributing moral blame. In fact, leniency creates two familiar traps. The problem begins when we try to explain the reasons for our leniency. We appear to have two options. If we say, *this is not your fault, so we are being lenient,* the child learns that he cannot control the behavior. Yet we expect him to learn to control some of it, so this is self-defeating. If we say, *we know you didn't mean anything by it, you'll try harder next time*, then we are attributing intention and setting the child up to fail: Trying harder may not yield any immediate gain, so when the child screws up again, he will feel he is taking advantage of our kindness. Thus leniency intensifies, rather than relieves, the implicit moral stakes. Using leniency can actually exacerbate the problem we're trying to solve, because it fails to avert the puzzle of attribution.

So the analogy of the parking ticket must not be taken to represent leniency. Instead, it must stand for firm, frequently issued consequences devoid of moral attribution. Such consequences could make a big difference in the lives of the attention-disordered, because our transgressions commonly provoke a reactive stance. When we act impulsively, forget things, or fail to carry out our responsibilities, we annoy and disappoint the people around us. Since we generally lack a good explanation for our behavior, the transgression seems even more outrageous. We have already seen that "I have ADHD" doesn't often function in the real world as an excuse. Our interlocutors worry, instead, that we didn't value them or their needs enough to remember them or act on their behalf. They resent us.

This resentment, and the moral responsibility it attributes, drives the question of our responsibility. That is the outcome we must avoid. When people with ADHD display their characteristic behaviors, we should issue the attention disordered the equivalent of parking tickets, rather than handing down criminal convictions. Better yet, when they avoid displaying symptoms, we must refrain from gratitude or other reactive responses, but instead devise and offer non-reactive forms of reward, which can merely be withheld when they display symptoms.

Non-reactive consequences answer those who worry about coddling the disordered—for non-reactive consequences are no less consequential for being non-reactive. They are consequential without trapping the attention disordered in an attributional puzzle. Reactive consequences harmfully insist that the transgressor truly and freely intended to transgress. To this, an attention disordered girl wants to say, "But you are wrong, I didn't mean to do it!"—and then wonder in perpetuity if she spoke truthfully or not. Non-reactive consequences say only, "Your behavioral control unit—as opposed to someone else's—directed this behavior, so we shall hold you accountable for it." To such a claim, the attention disordered need give no answer at all—merely an acceptance of the consequence. If she doesn't like the consequence, and can see a way to avoid the behavior in the future, nothing stops her from trying. If she cannot, she can accept this bit of misfortune the way a shortstop accepts a bad-hop grounder. No method of responding to a disorder can drive misfortune out of our lives, but misfortune is easier to deal with than blame.

This treatment of the attention disordered by others can also extend to the way the attention disordered regard themselves. We accomplish little trying to decide if we truly meant to park our car in the metered space, or if it was an accident of our nature. Better to pay the ticket, look for ways to avoid the problem in the future and, if these don't seem forthcoming, set aside some money to pay the expected fines.

The next chapter will offer parents of children with ADHD the practical tips they need for implementing this non-reactive model.

6 — Strategies for Parenting Non-Reactively

In this chapter, we will look at the problems that reactive parenting can cause for children with ADHD. For readers who are not parents, but cope with adult ADHD, I would encourage you to read this chapter closely, too. Childhood offers the richest expression of the disorder, and it was in childhood that we learned our own particular approaches to our disorder, including maladaptive approaches that remain with us today. Examining parenting also offers a special clarity, because a parent self-consciously strives to treat and accommodate the disorder, while bosses, co-workers, friends, and spouses may have little reason and/or ability to do so. The burden of coping with adult ADHD falls largely on the afflicted; we must parent ourselves. So, what kind of parent do we need?

As a parent, I learn as much about myself and my disorder as I do about my son and his disorder. Three swampy semesters past Algebra II, we realized that my son had long satisfied his college entry requirements, and could drop math and replace it with a harmless elective. When we figured it out, he was one week into the new semester, and had already fallen five assignments behind. We didn't tell our son outright, but encouraged him to figure it out by searching the college requirements online or asking his counselor. When he realized he could just drop the class, hand back the book, toss the missing assignments in the trash, and never do another, he had mixed feelings. "It feels like cheating," he said. I told him he didn't have to drop math, but that if he did, and he felt guilty about it, he could always do some more Spanish homework. By dropping math, he would open up space in his life to succeed at other things. Just the same, it was gratifying to hear him confess some guilt about dropping math. It made me feel like I had succeeded as a parent. After all, he showed no shame about falling five assignments behind, so it was nice to see he had a conscience about something.

My secret satisfaction when he revealed his guilt about dropping math stands as evidence both of my blinkered parenting and my son's need to hide his feelings. He had surely felt guilty about the five missing assignments, and about the many missing assignments that preceded them, but I didn't see it. My son had become a master at concealing guilt from me, for fear I would play upon it in an attempt to make him do his homework. He wanted to do his homework and be a good kid, but he didn't want me to make him do it—so he had to hide the lever of guilt from me, in (completely justified) fear that I would pull it. Part of that effort no doubt required hiding his guilt even from himself, which made it all the harder to face future assignments once he'd fallen behind.

This story serves to caution us against the weapon of shame, which, especially when parenting the attention disordered, is like chemical warfare: It is as likely as not to blow back into our own face. I try to avoid using shame in my parenting, but my son still feels guilty, and the effect is compounded when he hides his guilt from me.

So how can we encourage non-reactive strategies in our own parenting? I will first review some contemporary parenting methods to illustrate the difference between reactivity and non-reactivity. This will not be a comprehensive guide to parenting the child with ADHD, as parenting methods are varied, and new models are constantly being advanced (partly because anxious parents comprise a lucrative market for booksellers). But by examining a few popular methods, we can learn what to look for in evaluating any model, and in that way equip ourselves to choose models or techniques that will meet the needs of kids that require non-reactive parenting. Note that when we label a method "reactive," this does not impugn the method entirely, but merely indicates its unsuitability for use with characteristic or symptomatic ADHD behavior.

I will examine six parenting methods to see if and how these might work non-reactively:
- Modeling
- Moral Praise
- Descriptive Praise
- Communicative Parenting
- Natural Consequences
- Token Economy

Modeling
Modeling is by far the most powerful and often-overlooked parenting method. Using modeling means exhibiting the behavior we want to encourage in a child. It is a powerful tool for shaping behavior, and happily, it is non-reactive.

Exhibiting a behavior we want to encourage makes no attribution about whether or not a child intends or does not intend a behavior, whether or not the child happens to copy the modeled behavior. Modeling will not be as quick and effective when addressed to symptomatic behavior, but that just means we must use it patiently. I have clear memories of my mother's calendar that hung by the phone, her daily planner stretched out on the kitchen table, and the orderliness of our home. Of course, I ignored any daily planner she ever gave me, and joyfully kept my room in disorder. My mom reminded me of appointments, except in school, which she couldn't control and where I simply floundered. Beginning in my twenties, my wife—at that time my girlfriend—told me when I had things coming up, because I still kept no calendar. I really only learned to manage time using a calendar, and keep an orderly household, late in my thirties. Oddly, I now have less tolerance for clutter than my wife. I have had to learn to accept her stacks of work papers and folders on the hearth and the bench by the front door, which I would prefer to see stark and object-free. It took two decades for my mother's modeling to sink in and affect my behavior, but it is truly part of me.

Other than the patience required, the biggest problem using modeling with the attention disordered is staying calm. Suppose an attention-disordered child with impaired self-monitoring and planning skills fails to notice or anticipate his own hunger, omits his daily snack, sinks into low blood sugar, and a parent shows up to remind him of the chores he must do before his Aikido lesson, because today is Wednesday. A tantrum results. A skilled parent can greet the situation with equanimity, and model problem-solving by stepping outside the emotional context, diagnosing the problem, and solving it by replacing the chores with a snack. I confess I was not that parent, but my wife was, and eventually I improved at it myself.

The difficulty here is that ADHD symptoms in a son or daughter can be so frustrating to the parent that they trigger ADHD-like responses of emotional escalation in the parent; as a result, rather than modeling self-control and problem solving, the parent becomes a model of the undesirable behavior. In the novel *The House of God*, by Samuel Shem, a resident at a teaching hospital gives young interns advice I try to remember as a parent: "The first thing to do when a patient goes into cardiac arrest is to take your own pulse." Parents who can maintain an approach of calm problem-solving amidst the whirlwind of an ADHD child are giving that child a gift. It will pay off over a lifetime—even when the immediate results may not seem obvious. It occurs to me as I write this sentence that my mother modeled calm problem-solving for me as well, and I am often, though not always, able to emulate that now as an adult.

Moral Praise

While modeling is perfectly appropriate to the needs of a child with ADD, the second most natural, efficient, and pervasive parenting approach is not. What could come more naturally, when children misbehave, than scolding? When children behave well, what parent wouldn't show pride? This approach is so ubiquitous that it hardly needs a name, and parenting guides never claim to have innovated this approach. In the hands of a moderately skilled parent, it can work instantly from across a room, with a single word or gesture. Over-achieving parents find the method retains its power decades later, even from across the country. Yet this is precisely the approach that creates problems in the case of symptom-like behavior.

Both moral praise and scolding epitomize reactivity, because both attribute intent to their target. Contemporary parenting advice rightly favors praise over scolding, but moral praise offers little advantage over scolding for our purposes. Moral praise implies intention on the part of the child, so such praise undermines our goals as destructively as moral blame does. If we bestow moral praise when a child with ADHD appears to suppress a symptom, we send a covert message that the child can control this behavior. This becomes a set-up: The next time the child fails to suppress a symptom, the moral nature of the fault has already been attributed. How can it be morally to a child's credit to suppress a behavior unless it is a moral failure for him to exhibit it? Logic forms the link, and children can intuit it.

Descriptive Praise

Praise is immensely powerful, so we must find a way to praise non-reactively. I have included the term "moral" as a modifier for the wrong kind of praise for a reason: Praise need not be moral. One can attend to positive behaviors without labeling them as good, and children will accept this form of attentiveness to their efforts as praise. Howard Glasser, author of *Transforming the Difficult Child*, suggests merely describing the child's behavior to him or her, as carefully as possible and in a neutral tone. Here are some examples of descriptive praise:

- "I see yesterday's homework isn't in your backpack. You must have turned it in."

- "You are hanging up the towel in the bathroom."
- "You have been working for ten minutes and you are already on problem 12."

While this flat, laconic praise may sound strange to parents at first, Glasser finds that the children he works with prefer this to moral praise, which they seem to distrust. We can see why. Because children with ADHD justifiably fear they cannot really control their symptomatic behavior, they have good reason to fear moral praise. If they accept praise for being "good" this time, they logically open themselves to moral blame the next time. As a result, they cannot hear moral praise without fear, resentment, and cognitive dissonance—all of which can manifest as distrust and aversion to praise.

Descriptive praise offers an easy and potent method for using praise within a non-reactive approach. As a teacher who regularly uses this kind of praise with all the teens in my classroom, I can vouch that this kind of praise is just as powerful as moral praise, and often more so. When I point to a group and say, "This group has taken out their paper," the other table-groups take out their paper, and the praised group starts writing. Children—even teens—crave adult attention. They recognize the attention required to form a careful description of their behavior, and view it as a tangible form of attention. The technique works just as well with children in the home. The ornamental words we like to add to our descriptions, or use instead of descriptions—words like "Good job!" or "I am so proud of you!" or "Thank you!"—may seem like an intuitive and loving way to amplify praise, but such amplification doesn't boost the signal for the attention disordered—it only increases the noise.

Communicative Parenting

To widen our approach, we might consider "communicative parenting" strategies that progressive parents have favored for decades in place of scolding and punishment. This approach—exemplified by a book like *How to Talk So Kids Will Listen & Listen So Kids Will Talk* by Adele Faber and Elaine Mazlish—is rooted in the idea that children can be partners with parents in their own growth when parents learn to communicate with their children effectively. This means avoiding such common parental communicative tactics as shaming, moralizing, lecturing, and threatening. Instead, the parent should solicit and accept expressions of children's feelings, express their own feelings, describe behaviors, and seek to solve problems with children by talking to them. Much of Faber and Mazlish's book can be useful for parenting a child with ADD. They advocate "descriptive praise," just as Glasser does. They also encourage parents to allow children to face natural consequences, another useful technique we will examine shortly.

The underlying assumption of their approach, though, is as reactive as traditional parenting. If we do not examine this carefully, this reactivity will defeat our purposes. This approach to parenting rejects moralizing, and dispenses with scolding and lecturing in favor of a more democratic forum; in this way, children might figure as partners in growth and conflict resolution. But the idea of children partnering with parents suggests a kind of implicit moral compact. Why would children partner with parents to improve their behavior? Any answer to this question will likely posit a moral good in the child—whether this is a child's love for the parent, or commitment to harmony, or desire for improvement in accordance with parentally-modeled values. I do not object to any of this, but we seek a non-reactive method. We cannot overlook the moral compact at the heart of progressive parenting, for it holds the same peril for the attention disordered as does the overt moral preaching of conventional parenting.

The moral aspect of communicative parenting reveals itself in Faber and Mazlish's very first steps. When a child misbehaves, they urge parents to accept the child's feelings, and share their own. Why should parents share their feelings? Surely Faber and Mazlish assume, quite reasonably, that children care about their parents' feelings. But if a discipline process that begins with the sharing of feelings produces nothing more than a repeat of ADD symptoms, a question will insinuate itself: "Don't you care about mommy's feelings?" The parent may refrain from saying this out loud, but it is implicit in the logic of the process. If mommy's feelings matter—and why else would she share them?— behavior that causes bad feelings for mommy carries a moral burden. Such a moral breach raises exactly the question we want to avoid in parenting the attention disordered: "Did you do that on purpose?"

Other steps that Faber and Mazlish recommend as alternatives to punishment also rely implicitly on the child's assumed good intentions. They recommend that parents express "strong disapproval" of unwanted behavior. This makes sense for a child who willfully or even unknowingly misbehaves occasionally; it becomes problematic when a child with ADD seems unable to avoid exhibiting the same behavior over and over. If parents believe in the child's good faith, surely they must accept that after multiple restatements of disapproval that the child gets the message. Repeated expressions of disapproval for the same behavior cannot help but carry a message of resentment.

Similarly, another step involves offering the child a way, as Faber and Mazlish put it, "to make amends." The word "amends" implies moral failing. I do not regard this choice of words as accidental, but as intrinsic to an approach built on an implied moral compact between parent and child. We might suggest practical ways for a child to mitigate the consequences of her behavior, but this is very different from urging her to "make amends." Only with careful attention to such subtle distinctions can parents of children with ADD use the communicative approach to solve such problems as can be solved, while avoiding the pitfall of larding symptomatic behavior with moral weight.

Natural Consequences

If we expect the moral compact of a parent-child partnership to help treat ADD, we risk casting symptoms as moral threats to this partnership. This is the reactivity we are trying to avoid. Faber and Mazlish also recommend natural consequences, whereby parents allow the child to face outcomes that stem logically or naturally from behavior, rather than contriving arbitrary consequences. Natural consequences, if used appropriately, can work non-reactively. Consider a typical ADHD problem: getting dressed on time for school. For a distractible child, getting dressed can be an interminable process. A pure natural consequence might simply be letting the child show up late to school. This implies no moral censure or resentment on the part of the parent, so the child has no cause to puzzle over his moral responsibility for the lapse. But this example also indicates some possible problems with the approach. It is likely the tardy student will be scolded by his teacher, so what appears non-reactive is only a deferred reactivity. Worse, deferring a consequence is a poor practice for the attention disordered, as one of the most important symptoms of our disorder is our trouble orienting ourselves in time. A deferred consequence can be worse than no consequence, because it presents itself to us without a context, and therefore appears arbitrary.

Still, natural consequences have a potential virtue. If consequences appear with the impersonal quality of natural events, they carry no moral weight. If it rains and you have no umbrella, you get wet. This is not a punishment for a moral fault; it is merely a consequence. It is worth looking for ways to modify natural consequences in such a way as to preserve this prized non-reactive content while mitigating potential adverse aspects of the method. Rather than merely watching as the child arrives late to school for a probable scolding, for example, a parent could link the time it takes for the child to get dressed to her bedtime. Perhaps the prospect of a generous bedtime will motivate the child to get dressed faster, or perhaps the child will discover she prefers exchanging a late bedtime for a leisurely morning pace. Possibly the child will not manage to accord her behavior with the late bedtime she prefers. Whichever way this plays out, the problem is solved without moral judgment. The parent need not form any attribution of intent to explain why her child takes a long time to get dressed. Maybe she has ADHD, maybe she doesn't care enough about punctuality, or maybe she is engaging in Buddhist-like meditation on the significance of each separate article of clothing: It makes no difference with this approach. We can even strengthen this approach by using the problem solving of the communicative method. If parents and child agree together on the plan to modify bedtimes, it establishes the child's role as a partner in a way that won't be undermined by symptomatic behavior. The parent has no reason to be disappointed or to disapprove if, after agreeing on this response, the child gets dressed slowly. The joint problem solving did not ask the child to suppress symptoms, but merely to mitigate their consequences.

When natural consequences can be adopted, they are the very model of the "parking ticket" approach. Rather than the parent speaking in a voice of moral censure, the practice of natural consequences allows the parent to speak with the morally neutral tone of physical laws. Without saying a word, the parent delivers a mini-lecture: "Time is a finite resource. You can use it for getting dressed slowly, or, if you can get dressed quickly, you can use it for extra time before bed the night before." This contrasts with the very different moral message that good children get dressed on time.

The Token Economy

Unfortunately, natural consequences cannot always be adapted for every problem at every stage of development. Howard Glasser recommends using a positive token economy with the attention disordered. This can serve as another useful non-reactive parenting tool. In a positive token economy, children earn points or tokens by displaying listed behaviors, and spend the points on privileges. In a positive system, points are never taken away for bad behavior. Parents list the value of each behavior and privilege on a chart. Parents can charge points for virtually everything the child likes, and offer points for even the simplest of activities. Natural consequences can be challenging to arrange for each behavior, but tokens can be distributed for any desirable behavior. While making a chart and keeping tally can seem cumbersome, a currency for rewards in the home can be as useful and fluid as money in a market economy. It offers parents the power to offer non-reactive responses to any behavior, at any time. This can be especially valuable in turning around a situation that has deteriorated into a cycle of negativity. The child faces a chart full of ways to earn points, and by deciding which activities to pursue, he enlists in a positive movement toward change.

We used this method when our son was eight and things were at their worst. My wife had once worked with emotionally disturbed children in a residential treatment center, and when she found herself employing protective holds she learned at that job on our son, we both knew things had gotten out of hand. This was not just a question of ADD anymore, but of secondary symptoms of anger and defiance. At one point in this saga we removed the clothes from his closet and replaced them with one white shirt and one pair of blue pants; he would earn his clothes back, if he chose, with points. We made sure to offer plenty of opportunities for points, and he had them back within a day. We built quickly on his success by continuing to give him points and let him spend points for activities, keeping the balance positive so he could experience his efforts yielding positive results, again and again. This reestablished the positive link between effort and reward that had been severed by his ADHD, and by our resentful response to it. Under the point system, apparently symptomatic behavior does not occasion blame, but merely a lost chance at points.

For this to work, caregivers must run a token economy as a positive system. Elementary classrooms often use a negative point system in which the teacher writes the name of misbehaving students on the board, to be accompanied by checks for further misbehavior, and an eventual loss of privileges like recess. Children are likely to experience this negative system as reactive, with every check carrying an implied message of resentment. A positive system helps avoid this pitfall.

Of course, a parent can undermine the potential non-reactivity of this system through word or tone. If the parent offers reactive comments to accompany the points, the points assume a moral charge. Seemingly harmless and kind appraisals, (such as "Look how many points you have! Doesn't it feel good to behave so nicely?") invest the points with pride and judgment, replacing the moral neutrality we seek. As parents, we naturally want to express pride in our children, but we must reserve expressions of pride solely for behavior outside the scope of the disorder.

Some parents—and I was initially among them—resist the token economy idea because they fear it sends too mercenary a message, as though one must pay a child to behave. In this view, children should do good things because they care about themselves and others, not because they expect tangible rewards. This objection is misplaced in the context of ADHD. If the disorder is responsible for the behavior, then it does not matter whether the child cares about himself or others—he may display the behavior regardless. Attributing care or carelessness represents exactly the sort of moral attribution we should avoid. The impersonal, business-like quality of the tokens is a virtue for our purposes, not a liability.

Parents inclined to resist the token economy should remind themselves that they may indulge freely in more personal and humanistic moral motivation simply by reserving it for behavior unconnected with the disorder. If an attention-disordered child volunteers to do his sister's chores when she is ill, by all means, greet that with a warm hug and a moral endorsement of his caring behavior. *That* behavior had nothing to do with his disorder, so tossing a token at him really would be vulgar and dehumanizing. But an attention-disordered child who remembers to pick up his socks requires a token, *not* a hug. The hug sends the message that the child is lovable when he avoids symptoms. That is poison, because of what is implies about his lovability when he displays symptoms. The token states merely that he can gain rewards by engaging in specific behaviors. A proper understanding of reactivity allows the use of tokens alongside moral methods.

This insight helped me lose my fear that using tokens would produce a reward-seeking robot. As my son grew older, the easiest token to use becomes money. A clever person can figure out a way to monetize anything. Approaches that would once have seemed crass to me now seem like efficient ways to avoid the trap of reactivity. My son, at 14, wanted more freedom to handle his own decisions about homework. He had a homework packet he could finish at home, but he insisted that he should be allowed to complete it the next day in class, because the teacher would give them time. Because of his ADD, I distrusted his faith in this possibility. An argument ensued, and I cut the argument short by asking for a five-dollar deposit in return for letting him make his own decision. He would get his deposit back when I saw the work appear in the teacher's online grade book. He was happy to put down a deposit on his freedom—important to him at that age—and he got the money back the next day when he succeeded. Had he failed, he would have faced the non-reactive consequence of surrendering his deposit.

I used a similar deposit system to promote punctuality at his bass lessons. I would take a five-dollar deposit a half hour before the lesson to reserve the parental taxi; I would refund the deposit following a timely departure. Under this method, he would tell me to get in the car, rather than the other way around. Note that I did not pay him to take bass lessons. He took intrinsic joy in playing bass, so I did not want to turn that into a paid chore and undermine that intrinsic value. I did not pay him to do anything; I just took a deposit against tardiness. Punctuality is a challenge for the attention disordered, and the deposit ensures he has some skin in the game—skin, but no heart. I don't want his heart on the line in a punctuality game, because given his disorder, all the heart in the world might not be enough for him to win. He can survive the loss of a little skin. The point of non-reactive parenting is to make sure we never place our hearts on the line when the outcome may be determined by a disorder.

7 — Assertiveness: Defeating Reactivity as an Adult

When I moved to Los Angeles from the suburbs, I soon became frustrated with parking tickets. The first time I got one, I was angry, but I examined the sign and figured out what I had done wrong, and resolved to be more careful the next time. Then I got another, and another. I began to think there was something wrong with me, or with the city, or my luck. I was angry, and I kept getting angry, until I changed my approach.

I realized that in order to live any kind of normal life with a car in the city, I must expect a certain number of parking tickets. I did not become the rich man who ostentatiously ignores parking rules; I did the best I could to park legally. But I made a rule for myself: When I got a ticket, I would not get angry. Instead, as soon as I got home, I would dial the number on the back of the ticket, pay the ticket off with a credit card, and throw the ticket away. Then I would tell myself it was over. I lived in Los Angeles for ten years like this, getting no more or fewer tickets than anyone else, and not suffering much from them at all.

This is one approach an adult with ADHD must take to live with the disorder. The disorder affects behavior in familial, social, romantic, and professional worlds—which means a person with the disorder may frustrate people in every circle of life. For the most part, these people will not be nurturing parental figures who arrange to respond non-reactively. They will resent us, shame us, and blame us. We may know there is no point in trying to figure out if we really deserve blame. But we will be held culpable by others anyway, and we can hardly expect to diffuse the situation by handing people copies of Chapter 3 of this book. When we suffer setbacks and face resentment, we can start by handling it the way I learned to handle parking tickets: Pay the fine and move on.

If we have been raised to think that we should react to mistakes by dwelling on feelings of guilt or shame as a kind of atonement, or to protect against future mistakes, we should work actively against this tendency. It is counter-productive for us to ruminate on guilt. We should disavow the self-regarding reactivity of guilt or shame, parenting ourselves non-reactively.

Here are some examples of strategies we can use to pay the ticket and move on:

- After we arrive to work late, we resolve to put ourselves to bed earlier the next night, and set our alarm earlier.
- If we miss an appointment, reschedule at the convenience of the other party.
- Arrange with a flower shop to deliver flowers on an ongoing basis to loved ones on all the proper occasions each year: birthdays, anniversaries, etc.
- Alter the environment in which a symptom arises. Put things you need to remember to take with you next to the keys you need to drive; set yourself reminders; and ask people to text or email you requests, rather than just verbally mentioning them.
- Restructure commitments to shoulder more tasks that play to strengths, while shifting symptom-sensitive responsibilities to someone else, either by trading duties or hiring someone to help out.
- Sign up for automatic bill pay.
- Examine daily routines to see if a task we tend to forget could be linked to a particular moment when it would suggest itself logically.
- Streamline tasks that draw upon too many planning and attentional resources—deciding, for example, to eat the same thing for breakfast every day to simplify shopping.
- Trim unnecessary tasks from your life. If it doesn't have to be done, and you find it difficult to do or remember, decide once and for all just not to do it. I am a teacher, and sometimes the office sends a summons for a student whom I will only see later in the day. I no longer put it on my desk in the hope that I will remember to give it the student. I just throw it away. The office can send the summons when they need the student.
- Act quickly and decisively to modify our approach to problems, rather than letting them fester and create more guilt.

We imagine that guilt should prompt positive changes, but for the attention disordered it won't. Our characteristic behavior happens without our explicit consent, so we seldom have a chance to consult our moral convictions in time to act. Feeling guilt about characteristic ADHD behavior is worse than useless. We must channel the energy wasted on guilt into reshaping the environment in which we act. We must take active steps to reroute our workflow around the challenges caused by our disorder.

But these suggestions, and others like them, may not solve the problem entirely. We will still screw up in ways that startle, confuse, disappoint, and frustrate our bosses, family, colleagues, partners, and spouses. When we do, we will face their judgment. "It was my ADD" serves no more magical a function now than it did when we were kids. If we lack a better response, our struggle to engage in self-regarding non-reactivity will be imperiled by the reactivity around us. We cannot avoid internalizing the reactivity around us by a sheer act of will. We need a way to confront reactivity as adults, without falling into the trap of arguments or excuses.

Psychologist Manuel J. Smith begins his pioneering book on assertiveness, *When I Say No, I Feel Guilty*, with a provocative declaration. "You have the right," he announces, "to judge your own behavior, thoughts, and emotions, and to take the responsibility for their initiation and consequences upon yourself." This is the right we must insist upon. After all, we have a plan for judging our own actions—we will judge them non-reactively. We know how we must judge ourselves, but we need a way to prevent the reactive attitudes of others from seeping into our self-regard.

Smith does not expect that living the declaration he makes could be just a matter of saying it. He doesn't even suggest saying it. Nor does he suggest holding it as a belief through an effort of will. Instead, he explains how to behave as though it is the case. How can we do this when we are surrounded by people who consider our mistakes to be ample warrant for their reactive judgment? Smith's book recommends and demonstrates a set of communicative strategies that allow people to be their own judge in interactions with others. For us, this can serve as a guidebook for deflecting reactivity.

I have already partially drawn from Smith's book in my metaphor of getting parking tickets. Smith doesn't use this term as I have, but he tells a story about being given a traffic ticket, and his story inspired my metaphor. He recounts being ticketed for driving too slowly on the freeway. The officer scolds him, "If you want to be a putz in the slow lane, that's okay. But if you want to be a putz in the fast lane, that's wrong, so don't do it again." Smith views this as manipulative, because in addition to giving him a ticket, the officer wants him to feel guilty. Smith decides he will be his own judge, concludes that he doesn't need to accept guilt along with a ticket, and acts accordingly. He doesn't report which assertiveness method he uses in this encounter, only that the officer seemed disappointed when Smith didn't cower in the face of his scolding.

Readers of his book can surmise that Smith did not attempt to justify himself to the officer. Arguing would constitute a tacit admission that the officer has a right to judge Smith's behavior in addition to ticketing him. Debating our behavior implicitly cedes the right to others to judge us, because engaging in the argument assumes the other person's view matters enough that one must try to change it. If Smith is to be his own judge, then why would he need to change the officer's opinion? In Chapter 4, we saw that the most adaptive way to live with the puzzle of ADHD is to accept that other people may form their own attributions about our intentions, while asserting our own. Living this precept requires that we refrain from disputing others' attributions.

What do we do instead? Smith's method of assertiveness offers clues as to how he deflected moral blame for his slow driving. He may have simply declined to respond verbally to the officer's provocation. Instead, he may have merely gazed neutrally at the officer until the officer despaired of getting a rise and continued his process of ticketing. If the officer seemed to require a response, Smith may have summarized the officer's statement back to him, omitting the moral judgment and maintaining a neutral tone: "So you're saying the fast lane is for fast drivers." If the officer accepts this formulation, Smith can agree: He has stripped the moral blame away from the statement. But suppose the officer doubles down on moral blame. "Yes," the officer insists, "And only a putz drives slowly in the fast lane." Faced with an officer as persistently judgmental as this, Smith might respond by ceding the possibility that the officer may be right. "Yes, you may be right—only a putz would drive slowly in the fast lane." Although here Smith admits the officer may be right, he still doesn't seem to have internalized the officer's judgment. He hasn't performed shame. In fact, by seeming agreeable about the officer's opinion without performing any shame-behavior, he has withdrawn any option for the officer to gain an admission of shame from him. If the officer were to express what he feels at this point, he would have to say, "So you should feel like a putz, you putz!" To this, Smith might reply, "Yes, I probably should." Smith's behavior carries the message that while any number of facts or opinions might be ascribed to Smith and his driving, he reserves the right to judge for himself how he will feel about it.

This gives a good idea of how assertiveness works, but we cannot gain the full benefit from it by contemplating it. Just as a child gains nothing from a parent who reads about a parenting method without practicing it, we can only benefit from assertiveness by being assertive. I would urge my adult readers with ADD to get a copy of Smith's book, some other assertiveness training book, or to take a class in assertiveness. Only the actual practice of this method can reveal the extraordinary subtlety of the means by which we are induced to exhibit performances of guilt and shame. And this experience holds the magic. On paper, the problem of explaining our symptoms to other adults seems insoluble —a choice between admitting guilt and offering an excuse, when neither option is truly justifiable. We confront a false choice: to blush or to weasel. Assertiveness offers us a way to parse the imputation of guilt out of others' statements and respond in such a way as to neither accept nor reject it. I have found that doing this is deeply gratifying. It creates change from the outside in. By behaving assertively, one begins to change one's internal belief structure. I have come to truly believe it is my choice whether or not to accept guilt for my symptomatic behavior. The practice of assertiveness allows us to act as sole moral judge of our actions. As judges, and as readers of this book, we can see that the wisest and most practical approach is to accept only non-moral forms of responsibility for our characteristic behavior. Assertiveness makes this possible.

In behaving assertively, we can present ourselves as responsible, but not morally guilty. Merely telling ourselves not to feel guilty is not enough. Assertiveness behavior takes action to change the environment in which we live, and by changing our environment we bring about decisive change in the world within.

8 — Flow: The Power of ADHD

Parents filled half the bleachers at the football field, but there was no game that day. Down on the field the jazz band folded their chairs, while the marching band milled about on the sidelines, and the string orchestra sat arrayed in chairs on the field, looking incongruous among the wide white lines of the football field. A parent emcee standing at the front of the bleachers with a mic congratulated the jazz band for their performance and hawked raffle tickets to benefit the music program. Then he introduced the string orchestra. I wondered if we'd be able to hear them. The football field was a silly place for a string orchestra, but the music program used it once a year for the fundraiser, because that was the only venue that could accommodate the marching band. I looked over to spot my son, who was easy to find because, as the only kid on double bass, he was the only musician standing.

The teacher strode out and stood up on a box to conduct. After a few moments of giving directions, she raised her baton. She let it hang poised and motionless in the air for several beats, and then whipped it into action, her other hand describing shapes in the air. No sound came from the band. She bowed her head in mirth, and then turned to her right, facing the cellos and the bass. My wife covered her face with the program as the teacher carried on a short, mock-indignant conversation with our son, as the orchestra and the audience laughed. Apparently, this song was to have begun with only the bass playing. In that situation, if your bassist has turned to the wrong page in his sheet music, or his mind has drifted off, you find yourself waving silently in the air. The teacher tried again, and this time we all heard the notes from the bass ride clearly across the football field.

A year later, I would watch this same son play with an advanced regional orchestra. The performance featured some very difficult songs that would send my son and the other bassists racing up and down their fretboards. It also included a violin concerto featuring the associate concertmaster of the Los Angeles Philharmonic. I feared this would be its own sort of challenge for Tobias, because the score would call for the bass to sit out for lengthy rests while the violinist performed her magic, and then cut back in precisely in dramatic counterpoint. My son would face half a dozen chances to repeat the comedy of the football field, this time as tragedy. It was all too easy to imagine the violinist from the Philharmonic grimacing as my son cut into her solo with a misplaced slash of bass. I watched him anxiously for the first few rests. He would relax and look around, then lean into the score and poise his bow as his part came up, then charge in with the two other bassists. Soon I was able to relax as well, and almost forget it was my son up there and just give myself over to the music.

I don't think this was a question of learning from a mistake, or of luck. Tobias is a serious musician, and he took the fundraiser on the football field rather lightly. It was not so much a chance to devote himself to music as a kind of social occasion to share with his musician friends. The more advanced the performance was, in that sense, the easier it was for him. As the regional concert continued through a performance of a Dvorak's "New World" symphony, it became clear that my son was not going to make a mistake. He was wholly consumed by his playing. I thought how surprised his teachers would be to see him up there—this kid who couldn't take his homework out of his backpack when the other kids did, or remain focused long enough to outline a short chapter of a book—now a model of intense focus playing two hours of spirited, engaging, and challenging classical music.

Non-moral praise, natural consequences, the token economy, and creative monetization comprise an impressive array of non-reactive consequences for apparently symptomatic behavior in kids. We can modify our environment, choose our tasks to play to our strengths, and use assertiveness as an adult. But all this tries only to cope with our deficits, and the deficit model of the disorder fails to capture our strengths. To focus only on these techniques for controlling behavior and mitigating damage is to miss the entire beauty of life as those with ADHD experience it.

My exploration of reactivity in the context of ADHD is my own original contribution, but for this chapter, I will not say much that hasn't been said already by others, most notably John Ratey and Edward Hallowell in books like *Driven to Distraction*. I review their contribution here both because of its importance and because the rationale for it can be traced to Barkley's prevailing theory of the disorder in a way I am not sure has been noticed.

Recognizing our strengths requires us to understand and rely upon the special role intrinsic reward plays in the lives of those with ADHD. Intrinsic rewards are those that come from performing a task itself. People who truly enjoy creating music, reading about politics, practicing free throws, or programming a computer derive enjoyment from the activity itself, not from some reward or benefit that it brings. For example, I enjoy bicycling. Because I derive reward from the task itself, I need no external reward to ride a bicycle. On the other hand, I do not enjoy shooting free throws. To get me to shoot free throws, I would need to be given some kind of reward, like a dollar for every shot I made. In fact, given my lack of aptitude, I would demand remuneration for every shot *attempted*. This is an extrinsic reward, because it is not part of the task, but added to the task as a motivator.

I interpret Russell Barkley's model of ADHD to predict that those with this disorder would have trouble working for extrinsic motivators. For an extrinsic motivator to have force, one must periodically transfer attention from a task to the allure of the reward to motivate oneself to focus attention back on the unrewarding task. This requires executive function. People with ADHD cannot easily monitor our own motivational state, compare it to a long-range goal held in our working memory, and refocus our attention to gain an external reward that is separated from us by time (*ADHD and the Nature of Self-Control* 168–184). This does not mean that we cannot work for extrinsic rewards, but it suggests that such a motivator would need to be given virtually immediately, at the point of performance (*ADHD and the Nature of Self-Control* 343, *Executive Functions: What They Are, How They Work, and Why They Evolved* 205–206).

In the case of an intrinsically rewarding task, though, the reward flows from the task itself—so rather than having to transfer attention from the unrewarding task to contemplate the allure of an extrinsic reward held in working memory, and then back again, we need only let our attention flow where it takes us. The downside of this is obvious and familiar: It is hard to get the attention-disordered to do what others want us to do. But this also implies an under-appreciated upside: When it comes to following our true desires and doing what we *want* to do, we may actually be better at it than most other people. To my knowledge, this is not a conclusion Barkley has drawn, but it stems logically from his model. This may have eluded notice because we don't always remember how hard it can be for most people to immerse themselves in intrinsically rewarding tasks.

When people perform an intrinsically rewarding task that requires exceptional attentiveness, they face an overlooked challenge of attention allocation. Though the task is rewarding, one must still suppress certain impulses that conflict with the task. For example, people typically and automatically monitor their social environment. We find our social environment hard to ignore, even when focusing on an enjoyable task. As a teacher, I sometimes find that when I approach a small group of students conversing appropriately in a cooperative group, they freeze up when I come near. Their awareness of my presence in the social role of teacher disrupts their intrinsic focus, because they cannot help monitoring their own social performance of the role of student. Similarly, a couple that finds sex intrinsically motivating may still have trouble focusing on sex if their child is awake in the next room.

We also routinely attend to the passage of time. This explains the special quality of moments when we lose awareness of time, such as when immersed in a book or a movie. A loudly ticking clock forms a barrier to concentration when we read, as does an awareness of an impending appointment.

It is usually beneficial to apportion our attention between a task at hand and our background awareness of things like social cues or the passage of time. An effective warehouse supervisor, for example, can notice a pair of angry workers while scanning a jobsite in search of an empty pallet; this social alertness can allow her to avert a serious problem. An archivist cannot afford to lose track of time while examining an addition to the collection if there are other additions waiting to be inventoried on the loading dock. But certain tasks require complete attention if we wish to perform them at the highest level. A cellist would not do well to remember a doctor appointment during her concerto. A gymnast who notices his girlfriend talking to another guy in the audience may not give his best performance.

The psychologist Mihaly Csikszentmihalyi explains the special quality of attention exhibited by the cellist or the gymnast in his pioneering study of *flow*, which he defines as "the state in which people are so involved in an activity that nothing else seems to matter" (Csikszentmihalyi 4). He claims people are happiest when in this state of flow. In other words, it is an optimal state of intrinsic motivation. In order to maintain a state of flow, one must switch off certain automatic processes for monitoring ambient stimuli like time or social cues (Csikszentmihalyi 71). Given that he wrote an entire book about the topic, it would seem fair to say that he does not regard entering this state of consciousness to be easy for everyone. And indeed, he specifically notes two personality traits that inhibit flow: self-consciousness and self-centeredness. In his view, the self-conscious person remains too aware of social cues, and the self-centered person is too dependent upon extrinsic sources of reward (Csikszentmihalyi 84–85).

As a person with ADHD, I would say that relative to us, people without the disorder seem typified by exactly these traits: they are more likely than we are to be dependent upon social cues and extrinsic reward. I have consciously sought out friends who don't care what others think and do not rely on external validation; their excitement about their own, personal projects as musicians, artists, and actors seems so much more fulfilling. My son is even more dismissive of social imperatives and extrinsic rewards than I am, a trait which I both worry about and admire. No doubt he, like I did, will become more conditioned by these factors as he ages. Csikszentmihalyi recognizes that the attention disordered represent a personality type that stands in opposition to the self-conscious and the extrinsically motivated. Unfortunately, he also claims we are barred from achieving flow by our disorder (Csikszentmihalyi 84). On this claim, I think he, like others, misunderstands the disorder and is just empirically wrong. Since he cites no evidence for his claim, I suggest we defer to Ratey and Hallowell, who have worked intensively with the attention disordered as clinicians over many years, and have observed in them the trait they call "hyperfocus." I would also report, by way of anecdote, that writing this book demanded that this person with ADHD to engage in sustained, joyful concentration over a period of years—and that fact was, in fact, one reason I wrote it.

Csikszentmihalyi's mistake is failing to see that much of what others label "inattention" in people with ADD could better be described as "hyper-attention." People with ADD find it easy to enter a state of flow when engaged with our favorite thoughts and activities. Unfortunately, others often fail to recognize any upside to this. They become frustrated when we aren't attending to their needs, and we may become frustrated by their complaint. But it is not that we fail to attend to *anything*. We are often attending very closely to something—if only our *own* thought-train. If a child contemplates a bug in a windowsill during a math lesson or daydreams of comic book heroes when she is supposed to be getting dressed, others may not notice her success at focusing on these objects of fascination. But inside this child lies a seed of possibility. If she applies such focus to challenging activities that demand great skill, she will find herself wielding an advantage over those who struggle to turn off their extensively developed systems for monitoring such stimuli as time and social cues.

People with ADD often cherish and pursue activities offering intrinsic interest. We must recognize and make the most of this ability if we are to help the attention disordered reach their full potential. A daydreaming boy in a math class garners little praise. Yet we don't know what virtues that daydream might harbor or portend. He might be contemplating his history lesson, as I often did as a child. This is not daydreaming; it is a form of studying. When he gets an A on his history test—after neglecting to complete the homework for the same class—the history teacher may attribute his results to native cleverness. This may be flattering or dismissive, but either way, it mischaracterizes the basis of his success.

He succeeded by focusing on the problem, but in his own way, rather than through officially sanctioned but extraneous rituals of notes and flashcards. As a result, he takes blame for neglecting math, while perhaps failing to gain moral credit for his success in history, which the teacher may attribute to a morally neutral "natural aptitude." A better understanding of the special relationship the attention disordered have to intrinsically rewarding tasks should help us prevent these unfair and counterproductive attributions. We won't necessarily solve the child's problems in math by understanding the roots of his success in history, but offering the child the admiration he deserves for his fascination with history —rather than just writing it off as an innate ability for which he deserves no moral credit—better captures the means by which this child succeeds. It also grants him the moral recognition other children earn with their good grades.

The focused energy of an attention-disordered child offers power, and it begs to be channeled into the activity it craves. When attention-disordered children find success in a task to which they are intrinsically drawn, they create joy and success in a life which otherwise tends to fill up with other people's complaints about their inconvenient shortcomings. In pursuing intrinsically motivating tasks, they may discover the passion that will sustain them through childhood, or lead them to a career they love. In addition, by supporting attention-disordered children in their passions, we help them strengthen their abilities to focus and follow through on an endeavor, and some of this will transfer, eventually, to less intrinsically rewarding tasks.

This provides an invaluable key to success for adults with attention disorder. Adults find it much easier to choose an area of interest and pursue it. Primary and secondary schools expect students to practice a new occupation when the bell rings for each period: accountant, historian, grammarian, journalist, and scientist. The child must be his or her own executive secretary through it all, and it is exactly this administrative work that flummoxes those with ADD. As an adult, not only do workers have some choice over which occupation may suit them, they often have more control over how to approach their jobs. Certain tasks are anathema to a person with attention disorder, while others beckon. Adults thriving with the disorder do not force themselves to play uncongenial roles. Instead, we play to our strengths, throwing ourselves with our characteristic passion into careers we love and organizing our approach to the work in ways that avoid or minimize our weaknesses.

As we pay the emotional costs of our disorder—being blamed and resented, feeling shame, guilt, and confusion—we need to keep our eye on this big picture. We have things we love to do, and some of them even come with social or economic rewards. We can be better than anyone knows at these endeavors. It may take time for our devotion to pay off, but when they do, we gain rewards that those trained to respond to extrinsic motivation can only marvel at.

Conclusion: Free of the Puzzle

Some of the most fraught questions in raising an attention-disordered child or living an as adult with ADD stem from the puzzle this book has explored. The disorder seems to attract a plague of questions. As a parent of a child with ADD, we worry about everything:

- How much can I expect from my child?
- Why does my child frustrate me so much?
- Why does he do these things?
- Is this behavior truly out of his control, or could he try harder?

All this tempts us to conclude: *Maybe it's all his fault.* But more questions follow:

- Why can't his teachers tailor their instruction to his needs?
- Why does the world demand such unnecessary things from him?
- Don't people see the good things in him?
- Why can't I control my own resentment towards him?

Leading us to wonder: *Maybe it's all our fault.*
Meanwhile, those of us who have ADD ask ourselves:

- What do I say to people when they ask me why I did what I did?
- Was it my fault—or was it just my disorder?
- Could I just be bringing these problems on myself?
- Am I just using ADD as an excuse?

So we wonder: *Maybe it's all my fault.* On the other hand:

- Am I really that bad?
- Aren't my teachers (or bosses) just too picky?
- Couldn't people lighten up on these details and see the big picture?
- Can't I just be allowed to do the things I'm good at?
- Why does the world obsess over tiny details, and care so little about the

excitement of what really matters?

* Why must we measure out our life with coffee spoons?

It must be all their fault.

Questions of fault send us to the wrong place for answers. These questions seem to point inside our minds, as if the fact of our true intentions could be found in there. This is a false lead, because the question of what we intend cannot be answered as a fact, the the search for an answer to that kind of a question need never end. Answers to questions about intention are always open to more questions.

The philosopher Ludwig Wittgenstein said the purpose of philosophy is to show the fly the way out of the bottle. In living with ADD, we become this fly whenever we try to decide whether to blame a *disorder* or a *person* for a behavior. We flit about madly and run into barriers we cannot even see.

To find our way out of the bottle we must become aware of the uselessness and counter-productivity of reacting to apparently symptomatic behavior in moral terms. We must realize that simply by avoiding moral reactivity in the context of our characteristic behavior, we avoid the fate of the fly in the bottle. This doesn't mean we cannot live as moral beings, or treat the attention disordered as moral beings. Much of what we do fits no symptom, so this behavior remains available for moral treatment. Likewise, we need not offer a free pass for symptomatic behavior, for once we understand the difference between reactive and non-reactive consequences, then we can simply substitute non-moral consequences for moral ones. As parents, we can use modeling, non-reactive praise, natural consequences, and token economies. Adults with the disorder can recognize the counter-productive futility of moral censure in the context of the disorder. We can learn to employ assertiveness to deflect moral blame for apparent symptoms, while still accepting non-moral forms of responsibility for our actions.

When we leave the fly-bottle of our puzzling intentions behind, we free ourselves of needless confusion and shame. Outside the bottle, we will not be entirely free. All of us, ordered and disordered alike, can be encumbered by our own flaws. But the message of this book is that we must avoid adding to this a palpable but nearly invisible layer of shame, resentment, guilt, and confusion—feelings fostered not so much by a disorder but by a potent and pervasive misconception about the concept of intention.

Avoiding this misconception clears a space for us to nurture our best qualities, especially those stemming from the disorder itself, like the passion we bring to the activities that drive and sustain us, and our ease at entering a state of flow. Only by freeing ourselves of the puzzle of intention can we cut the problems related to our disorder down to the size of the simple, human obstacles that both critics of the disorder and advocates of those with the disorder want them to be.